The Essence of
SHINTO

Japan's Spiritual Heart

Motohisa Yamakage

TRANSLATORS

Mineko S. Gillespie
Gerald L. Gillespie
Yoshitsugu Komuro

EDITORS

Paul de Leeuw
Aidan Rankin

KODANSHA USA

NOTE FROM THE PUBLISHER:

The names of modern and contemporary Japanese appear in the Western order, while those of historical figures (pre-1868) are written in the traditional order: surname preceding given name.

For reference, the following chart shows those periods of Japanese history which will be most relevant to the discussion:

PERIOD NAME APPROXIMATE DATES (A.D.)

Nara	710–784	Azuchi-Momoyama	1573–1600
Heian	794–1192	Edo	1600–1868
Kamakura	1192–1333	Meiji	1868–1912
Muromachi	1336–1573	Taisho	1912–1926
Nanbokucho	1336–1392	Showa	1926–1989
Sengoku	1467–1568	Heisei	1989–

(Historians do not agree on exactly when the various periods started and ended, so the dates listed are approximate. Japanese writing often refers as well to *nengo*, or shorter periods named after each reigning emperor. Some of these will be introduced where relevant.)

Originally published in Japanese as *Shinto no Shinpi* by Shunjusha in 2000.

Published by Kodansha USA, Inc.
451 Park Avenue South
New York, NY 10016

Distributed in the United Kingdom and continental Europe
by Kodansha Europe Ltd.

First published in Japan in 2006 by Kodansha International
First US edition 2012 by Kodansha USA
22 21 20 19 18   5 4

The Library of Congress has cataloged the earlier printing as follows.

Library of Congress Cataloging-in-Publication Data

Yamakage, Motohisa, 1925-
    [Shinto no shinpi. English]
    The essence of Shinto : Japan's spiritual heart / Motohisa Yamakage ; translators Mineko S. Gillespie, Gerald L. Gillespie, Yoshitsugu Komuro ; editors Paul de Leeuw, Aidan Rankin.
        p. cm.
    Includes bibliographical references.
    ISBN-13: 978-4-7700-3044-3
    ISBN-10: 4-7700-3044-4
1. Shinto--Doctrines. 2. Spiritual lilfe--Shinto. I. Leeuw, Paul de, 1947- II. Rankin, Aidan, 1966- III. Title.
    BL2221.Y355613 2007
    299.5'61--dc22
                                    2006035866

www.kodanshausa.com

Calligraphy by the author: "*seimei* (clean bright)"

Table of Contents

Preface

The aim of this book is to express the essence of Shinto, especially its spiritual aspects, in terms readily accessible to the interested reader.

The word "Shinto" inevitably conjures images of a shrine for most people. For them, the shrine is a place where people go for seasonal festivals, offer prayers, worship Kami, or undergo the 7–5–3 (*shichi-go-san*) rite of passage.[1] The role of the shrine extends to more mundane, but no less crucial, areas of life. Charm cards are issued to give confidence to those taking examinations, for instance, or to give drivers a psycho-spiritual defense against the dangers of the road. People of all creeds—and none—will congregate at Shinto shrines to see in the new year. Shrines in the modern era provide for a wide range of individual and collective needs, some of them overtly spiritual or "religious" in character, others more subtly so, reflecting the spirituality of everyday life, underlying all aspects of human experience. This union of the sacred and the mundane is a distinctive feature of Shinto.

The essence of Shinto is found in our relationship and interdependence with Kami. Or to put it another way, Shinto is the path through which we seek to realize ourselves fully as human beings by acquiring the noble characteristics of Kami. This possibility is open to all men and women, but we must first become attuned to the spirit of Kami, which is itself identical to the essence of Shinto.

In our troubled modern era, materialism is the dominant force, and so talk of the invisible world, the realm of the spirit, is not always well received. Shinto, however, would not be complete without this aspect of mystery. There is much evidence, especially in supposedly advanced societies such as Japan and the West, of a growing dissatisfaction with the purely material and the narrowly rational, and a resulting hunger for the mysterious coupled with a desire to reconnect with the spiritual realm. As an evolving, organic system of spiritual values, Shinto is well equipped to satisfy these basic human needs.

At this point, *koshinto*, which means "the original Shinto of ancient times," becomes particularly important. *Koshinto* promotes the independent spiritual/mental training of each person for the improvement of their own character. Through *koshinto*, a systematic method of training has been handed down from ancient times. The institutionalized shrine exists for ritual services and prayers that reflect the rhythms of everyday life. Out of necessity, it responds to immediate and practical concerns, rather than providing the seeker with a systematic method of mental and spiritual cultivation. *Koshinto*, by contrast, allows the seeker to reach beneath the ritualized surface, to understand what Shinto really is, and be touched by the light of the spirit of Kami.

Koshinto, or Yamakage Shinto, has been handed down to me through many generations. Yamakage Shinto contains within it knowledge of ceremony, manners, rituals, methods of divination, traditional medicine, among an array of other things. It is an inclusive and comprehensive form of knowledge, of which this book touches upon only a few themes. The purpose is to give the reader an overview and so equip him or her for further practice or mental training. For example, I do not discuss in detail the procedures for ritual services and prayers for Kami, because these are available elsewhere. The ancient history of *koshinto* is also largely omitted from the text.

Shinto is the consciousness underlying the Japanese mentality, the foundation for Japanese culture and values. Japanese society is still in a state of confusion, one of the symptoms of which has been the proliferation of bizarre cults and sects. It is important, therefore, for the Japanese people to rediscover their spiritual essence and their cultural roots, and to make these a force for the good of humanity as a whole. I sincerely hope that my book will help achieve this aim.

Caring for the spirit of nature

In recent years there has been much talk of climate change and the disastrous consequences of human impact on the environment. We are constantly urged to limit our consumption of fossil fuels and live more respectfully with nature. This practical task of responding to the ecological crisis is given an ethical underpinning by Shinto, which from ancient times has seen it as the principal duty of human beings to care for and preserve their environment—to live within nature rather than attempting to dominate or destroy it. In Shinto, heaven, earth, and humanity are different manifestations of one life energy.

From earliest times, Japan has endeavored to preserve and nurture its abundant forests. Yet at times of upheaval and change, the forests have been damaged recklessly. Whenever this has happened, Shinto leaders have been at the forefront of campaigns to restore the forests, recognizing that they are the lungs of the nation and indeed the world. Japan suffered a tremendous loss of trees in the aftermath of World War II. This damage reflected the trauma of the people and the shift from spiritual toward materialistic values. Yet the importance of the forest, at both psychic and ecological levels, was understood by the Showa Emperor, who threw part of his personal fortune behind an appeal for reforestation. The people responded well and saw it as their task to restore the image of their country as a landscape of green mountains. As a result, with 9,600,000 hectares, Japan now ranks third on the list of most successfully reforested countries in the world.

Water will continue to run from mountain springs as long as we keep the forests intact. People in the West are now ready to see the world as Gaia, the ancient Greek goddess of the earth, a living organism, all parts of which are connected to and dependent upon each other. And as with other living organisms, when one part is injured or out of control, the whole loses its balance and becomes sick. When the earth becomes sick, we are obliged to use our knowledge and power to restore it.

An outward expression of Shinto's concern for the health of nature can be seen in the forested areas surrounding Shinto shrines. For more than three thousand years, the Japanese have believed that Kami, the powers of the spiritual dimension, can make contact with human beings through trees. We can therefore also find sacred trees within the precincts of certain Shinto shrines. Some of these trees are more than four thousand years old. A sense of the sacred in trees, and a desire to nurture them, is profoundly rooted in the spirituality of Japan.

Here we can find in Shinto a universal meaning and a practical ethos for today's world. It can attune us to see the connection between the well-being of the natural world and our own spiritual well-being. In the ancient wisdom of Japan, we can find a missing link that restores our awareness of nature, and so give us the wholeness we crave for in a world dominated by material and mechanical notions of progress. In the present practice of tree planting and arboriculture, we find a modern expression of an age-old spiritual sensibility.

Shinto is an authentic, indigenous spiritual tradition of the Japanese people. Many of its outward forms and practices are therefore specific to Japan, but its essence is valid for all of humanity and very relevant to us in our present predicament. Shinto's understanding of the intrinsic value of the natural world is linked to an emphasis on purification, which has a dual physical and spiritual significance. At the core of the Shinto tradition is the practice of immersing the body in water. Whilst this ritual is one of physical cleansing—the purification of the body—

it also represents the purification of the mind and spirit. It reminds us of the significance of water as the source of life, without which no life can be sustained.

In our urbanized culture, nature is often treated as if it were a mere wilderness, an occasional refuge for us perhaps, but not of central importance to our lives. The return of the idea of Gaia is a radical challenge to this way of looking at the world. It reminds us that we are part of nature, rather than above or beyond it. The water with which we purify ourselves is, after all, the first ingredient of the human organism. Gaia was entrusted with the preservation of nature's balance. She has living counterparts in Shinto—*Kunitokotachi no kami* and *Toyoukehime no kami*; the Kami of natural energy. Every creature comes into existence as if it is generated by its respect for the Kami of nature. Since these two Kami hide their presence behind their innumerable offspring, they are known as the invisible Kami. Yet theirs are the threads that hold together the great web of life.

Motohisa Yamakage

CHAPTER 1

Shinto for the New Millennium

Times are changing

We are living in a great historical period. Thousands of years have passed since human civilization introduced the use of written language, but the scale of technological and cultural change over the last two centuries is quite unprecedented. Today, different races and cultures continuously interact with each other and information circulates around the whole world within the blink of an eye, or the click of a mouse. Material and technological progress has been truly remarkable. This is due in large part to scientific advances, which have transformed our lives and at the same time changed our consciousness, our way of looking at the world. Modern humanity's knowledge of its own nature has leaped forward, along with our understanding of the earth and the structure of the universe. Whereas the ancients had powerful intuitions and insights, we have scientific facts. Such developments, scientific and material, are bound to have a transforming effect and touch all aspects of our lives.

It therefore seems strange to many that only religion has continued to transmit the same teachings largely unaltered, in many cases, for millennia. Only religion claims to have golden rules that can withstand scientific scrutiny. Certainly, there are some arguments in religion's favor. Religious teachings provide continuity amid change and a sense of history. They have survived past challenges and stood the test of time. Furthermore, the human mind and its awareness of spiritual values have remained constant.

These are all valid arguments for traditional religious belief and practice. Since I belong to the 79th generation of an ancient Shinto tradition, it is quite understandable that I attach great importance to tradition and continuity. However, I also believe that religious expressions, that is to say the language and form of religion, must adapt and evolve. There is now so much exchange of ideas between cultures and faiths that traditional forms can no longer be justified on grounds of tradition alone. Social and cultural changes have been so profound that the old forms often lack relevance to modern men and women. Therefore, we should not hesitate to make up for what we lack and to improve what we need to improve. To believe that only the language and form of two millennia ago are valid for today is pure bigotry and dogmatism, and far removed from any kind of spiritual awareness.

It is hard to deny that we live in an age of science and reason. People are trained to think rationally and place their faith in continual progress rather than timeless truth. We can, however, point out that human reason has its limits. Rationalism and positivism—the belief in inevitable progress—both provide only partial explanations for the human condition, or humanity's place on earth and in the cosmos. However these are not sufficient excuses for anyone who fails to engage with of other realities comes from their heart and their own experience.

That is why the importance of *chinkon* in Shinto has been emphasized repeatedly since ancient times. *Chinkon* is different from simple mental concentration or the quieting of the mind. Through the practice of *chinkon* one can actually break through the wall of other dimensions existing in their mind. When this happens, the other world will appear, and they will become aware of the worlds of spirit and Kami. Without this, people cannot approach Kami filled with reverence and awe, nor can they experience true faith with gratitude in their hearts and minds. However, the faith I am talking about here is not something that can simply be taught at college.

Thus, just as many Buddhist monks have seemingly become monks only for the sake of conducting funeral rites, many Shinto priests have become mere administrators and caretakers of shrines or performers of wedding ceremonies. I do not want to say that they should not conduct these important business affairs or preside over these profound human rites of passage. I only wish for them to wake up and rediscover the significance of rigorous exercises like *misogi* (see Chapter 4) or *chinkon* (see Chapter 8), and to embed these spiritual perspectives in their working lives.

Revival of original Shinto

Young priests become immersed in modern trends and look down on the spiritual aspect of faith, because they do not have any real spiritual experience. Leading persons of Shinto also become timeservers and merely reflect the times they live in, rather than positively engaging with them. When priests speak publicly about psychic sensibility or spiritual experience they are rarely taken seriously or appreciated, and often stigmatized as eccentric. I have heard, for instance, that it is taboo for priests to talk much about faith, even in the Ise Shrine. At Ise, the most important Shinto shrine in Japan, it is considered problematic if the priest has faith. People are not permitted either to have or to talk about mystical experiences through responding to the spirit of Kami with all their senses. This being the case, I would consider that the shrine is effectively no longer a religious facility. The priests at Ise pray on behalf of visitors for traffic safety or the healing of disease, but their prayers will not connect to the higher world because they do not believe in that world. These prayers offer no true consolation, and are thus fraudulent.

On the other hand, it is improper to overrate any mystical experience or psychic power or to use such powers for commercial ends. But we must also consider two obvious truths. First, mystical phenomena are essentially inseparable from the shrine. This will become evident in Chapter 3, where I describe the founding of a shrine. Secondly, the shrine and the parishioner are connected to each other in a spiritual relationship. Faith in the shrine is sustained by the mentality of *okage*, which means the assistance or protection of Kami or Buddha, as well as a sense of indebtedness and gratitude. If, however, a believer indulges in fake spirituality, or the misuse of psychic power, then the priest should have the ability to correct such errors. It is impossible to attain this ability from mere knowledge alone. It must come from spiritual training and work done by the priest himself.

Nowadays people feel an ever-greater spiritual thirst, but the place where the light of spirit of Kami shines is lost to them. Priests should not be allowed to drift aimlessly through ritual services that are devoid of actual experiences or knowledge of the faith underlying the practices. It is time for a call for the fundamental awakening of the Shinto establishment in Japan.

Exchange and co-existence among religions

Throughout human history, religion has fought countless wars and repeated many tragic massacres in the name of its great cause. This pattern continues even—perhaps especially—today. This is a difficult problem that never ceases to agonize and torment thoughtful religious people. However, it is unthinkable that religion—at least in the form of people's sense of nature and the presence of Kami—could disappear from this world, and we could not make it disappear even if we wished to do so. Furthermore, it is no longer permissible that single religions compete for sole dominance over others, especially in this so-called global era of growing cultural exchanges and an increasing interdependence. Even in the Western world, where Christianity for a long time has claimed to possess the one absolute truth, the existence and validity of other religions has been acknowledged and inter-faith dialogues have begun in earnest. Nowadays it is essential that all religions co-exist and interact. This can be achieved by respecting each other's similarities and differences while keeping our own faith. But if we find things to learn from each other's traditions, let us do so without inhibition.

In practice, this is not as easy as it sounds, and it becomes impossible to proceed in this way when a society does not provide the means for its members to grow and mature in a spiritual sense. It is likely that the human state of mind has not evolved sufficiently to reach this high level of consciousness. Furthermore, if human beings truly advance to a higher level, it may be that they will no longer need any particular religion, but will be able to follow their own path in their search for Kami.

The idea of child-spirit (*bunrei*)

From a universal point of view, I believe that Shinto can contribute something vital to the development of religion as a philosophy of nature.

One of the most notable Shinto philosophical principles is the idea of child-spirit (*bunrei*).[2] In Chapter 5, I shall explore in what sense human beings are the children of Kami, or better, how we have a full-fledged potential to become Kami. Shinto sees everything in existence as generated by and transformed from the ultimate origin of life; this is expressed in the idea that all forms of life are a child-spirit of the original Kami. This idea is also mentioned in the first chapter of the *Kojiki*, the Ancient Chronicles of Japan. This first chapter deals with the origin of (Japanese) history that is still shrouded in mythology. It mentions the coming into existence of three creator Kami who transformed and created themselves to bring forth various Kami, all of whom are child-spirits of these three creators. In their turn, these various Kami also transformed and generated their own child-spirits. Following this, these new child-spirits further transformed and generated all phenomena in the universe.

From this chain of procreation it may be inferred that in their innermost essence, human beings, animals, plants, and all natural matter are the offspring of the great original spirit Kami of the universe. Or put another way, everything comes to existence as a child-spirit of the original Kami. This core-spirit is also called *naohinomitama*. The meaning of making a ceremony and offering prayers and dedications of food to Kami is none other than expressing the awareness that we owe our life and sustaining life energy from the great source of nature, which is another name for Kami. As a result of increasing our awareness that we receive everything as a grace of Kami, we might get a clearer perception of *naohinomitama*, as the child-spirit of the great original spirit dwelling within all of us.

This idea of a child-spirit is not abstract academic theory. In fact, most of the shrines in Japan have developed by being respectfully dedicated to a child-spirit. The shrines dedicated to influential Kami, such as the Kami of Ise, Izumo, Suwa, or Hiyoshi are scattered all over Japan. This means that many places receive a child-spirit from the main shrine, and local people dedicate the child-spirit to their local shrine and pray for protection. The *ofuda* (a paper or wooden card on which the name of a Kami is written), which is kept in a Japanese *kamidana*, or household shrine, can be considered as another example of the tradition of paying respect to the child-spirit.[3]

Each Kami has its own characteristics, but they are not fixed. Furthermore, the Kami can spread out simultaneously into various places and various existences. This concept can actually be applied to human beings also. In the section on "one spirit, four souls" (Chapter 6), we shall see that the human being is the assembled body of many souls. This assembled body of souls can sometimes be divided. That is why a well-trained spiritual person can send off his own separated soul to a distant location or a different time period to perform long distance healing, precognition, or clairvoyance.

A Japanese scholar, Shinobu Origuchi, presents his beautiful interpretation of the birth of ancient scenery songs as follows:

> *When a man leaves for a journey, he leaves one of his souls to a woman staying at home, and the woman puts one of her souls in his charge. The man comforts his woman by singing a song to her soul that he has brought with him, and this song is about the scene he sees while on his journey. This is the birth of scenery songs.*

From a logical point of view this might appear as something mysterious and magical. However, it has always been a very important philosophical and spiritual principle:

"One is many—and many is one."
This is a very important philosophical principle that enables us to break through ordinary interpretations of the universe.

Reverence toward nature

Shinto teaches to revere "Great Nature." That means that everything in nature is the transformation and creation of Kami, therefore the sacredness of Kami dwells within it. As part of their everyday lives, and without recourse to complex philosophy, the Japanese people have loved and revered nature as a gift from Kami since ancient times. We have felt that plants and animals, as well as mountains and rivers, have lived with us and have been deeply connected to us. This love and reverence toward nature is a quality that should be reinstalled in our hearts, if we want mankind and earth to survive the ecological crisis that has resulted from excessive materialism.

Recently some scientists, notably the British geophysicist James Lovelock, have rediscovered the notion of "*Gaia*."[4] In this view the natural environment of earth is not seen as just a mechanical system, but more than that, as a highly organic network created by complex relationships and subtle connections between all forms of life. Life has therefore neither passively adapted itself to the earth's environment, nor been created by chance. Every life form, every creature has influenced the environment and helped to shape it. It has interacted with and depended upon other creatures as part of a harmonious cycle of creation. The world of nature is ultimately self-regulating and self-renewing, preserving its own order or homeostasis, restoring the planet's balance much like the immune system of an individual organism. We can therefore think of the earth as if it were a single organism, or the sum total of all living organisms: a self-regulating, self-rejuvenating biosphere.

Of late we have heard extensive use of the word "co-existence." This means that no creature can operate without regard for fellow-creatures. It can only exist and survive in a state of balance with other living organisms. Nature is the constant interplay of living organisms. It is the continuous search for and restoration of balance.

These perceptions of organic nature are identical to those that the Japanese have entertained and cherished deeply since ancient times. The islanders blessed with a rich natural world recognized intuitively that even plants and trees speak and that human beings could not live without mountains and rivers. In Japan's past there was no thought of conquering nature or of unilaterally exploiting it.

In Shinto, people sensed the dwelling place for Kami in the beautiful rocks or mountains, and they considered the *sakaki*, an evergreen leaf tree, as the *yorishiro*[5] for Kami. Therefore Shinto would never have been brought into existence without this love and reverence toward Nature.

Japanese Buddhist sayings, such as "mountains, rivers, plants, and trees will all become Buddha," or "the shape of the mountain and the sound of the valley stream are also the manifestations of Buddha" are expressions, in Buddhist fashion, of this Japanese spiritual sense of nature. It is a sensibility that is alive at the deepest levels of Japanese consciousness, although in modern times more and more Japanese are losing this sense.

Variety of religious perception

The sensitivity through which Japanese people can see the vital energy of Kami in all of nature is also rich in spirituality, since it feels and perceives various kinds of spirits. From a Western point of view this way of perception is called pantheism or animism, which means a way that perceives the spirit in every living organism or natural formation. Modern Japanese, who are influenced by the Western way of thinking, are inclined to dismiss this pantheism as primitive or barbaric. Meanwhile, the great religions of the West, which aspire to the supreme, the absolute god, the great original *chi*, or the absolute law, are in crisis or decline. This is because they are suffocating from a lack of spiritual breath. In reaction to this rigid religious system—and the limits of materialistic humanism—the West has seen the rise of various spiritual movements, like theosophy, anthroposophy, spiritual humanism, or the New Age in order to stimulate spiritual and mental growth. In those movements, men and women have begun to reveal the works of various spirits' existence that lead human beings to the light. People in those movements also claim that we need to retrieve and revive the spiritual way of looking at nature. These claims go well with the practice of ancient Shinto.

We should be able to contribute to those movements with Shinto's rich treasure. We have accumulated this treasure through many centuries of practice, based on a perception of spirit-soul and a sense of the spiritual world. I believe that this Shinto can respond to the demands of young people who are thirsting spiritually, and become a useful recourse against dangers on the spiritual path.

The flexibility and tolerance of Shinto

The other aspects of Shinto that respond well to the needs of this age are its exceptional flexibility and magnanimity. As I shall explain in the next chapter, Shinto does not have any fixed point of view regarding a founder, doctrine, precept, or image (object) of worship. Shinto has nothing to do with any of the dogmas that point toward absolutism.

Shinto values can be summarized as follows: first, how each person makes contact with the noble spirit of Kami; second, how each person shows gratitude and respect toward Kami; and third, how each person grows spiritually, by acquiring qualities that are the result of his or her contact with and reverence toward Kami.

Furthermore, considering the present situation in which many religions meet and co-exist, the aversion to dogmatism found in Shinto might be a model for religion in the global era. Kami exists beyond any human intellect or expression. Each specific religious system is but a fragment when viewed from the grand wisdom of Kami.

In other words, all teachings are as one. Every religion should be aware of this underlying truth. Even if Shinto seems far from the western concept of religion, it is a solid religious organism, and offers a path to Kami to men and women of all traditions and backgrounds. It is my heartfelt wish that many readers will understand and appreciate the essence of Shinto; in addition I sincerely hope some readers will use the essence of Shinto as the next step to a spiritual culture for all humanity.

CHAPTER 2

What is Shinto?

Shinto is a religion unique to the Japanese people

Shinto is undeniably a religion unique to the Japanese people. It is a natural religion born and nurtured in the Japanese islands, unlike Buddhism or Christianity, which are world religions that have come to Japan from foreign countries.

Certainly we cannot deny the influences on Shinto from Buddhism, Confucianism, or Chinese culture. Their influences on Shinto have been very distinctive, particularly in the area of language. This is so because from the third century onwards the influence of foreign cultures led to the introduction of a written script, and with that a grammatical structure and a system of philosophical reasoning.

This is why it is often said that Shinto has no identity of its own—that it is simply a combination of influences from outside countries.

Others say that Shinto is just old Japanese manners and customs. Many foreigners visiting Japan are moved when they witness the traditional festivals and visit the shrines. So they naturally ask, "what is the meaning of this?" Usually they end up getting ambiguous answers, such as "we are doing this because we have always done this—this is our ancestral tradition." Or they might simply be told that "we are supposed to do this," without any reason being offered for exactly why. So it is not unusual to find Shinto characterized as merely a series of manners and customs. Inquirers quickly discover that most Japanese don't have a clear way of explaining Shinto's view of the world or what Shinto really *is*.

Shinto, however, certainly has its own way of thinking and feeling as well as its own distinctive world view that cannot be adequately contained within the western concept of religion. Underneath an array of expressions that ostensibly have no pattern, Shinto is filled with a rich world of faith.

This aspect of Shinto, I believe, makes it especially worthy of consideration in a modern age when religion, in its conventional forms, has lost much of its attraction and influence.

What, therefore, is Shinto? In order to answer that question, we need to immerse ourselves deeply into the Shinto world, particularly *koshinto*, the original form of Shinto, its ancient spirit, which has remained unchanged by either historical or political manipulation.

According to the Western conception of religion, a religion typically has a founder, a doctrine, precepts or commandments, and objects of worship, such as symbols or idols. Shinto, by contrast, has none of these. This makes it radically different from religion as it is now commonly understood.

Let us therefore first consider the implications of a religion without a founder.

Shinto has no founder

Shinto is not a faith transmitted by a teacher to his followers. There is no equivalent of Gautama Buddha in Buddhism, Jesus in Christianity, or Mohammed in Islam. Historically, some Shinto sects such as "Watarai Shinto" and "Yoshida Shinto" were actually created and founded by certain people, but this does not mean these people were founders of Shinto. Instead, Shinto is a religion that has evolved out of the life and experience of the Japanese people. It has been shaped and nurtured by countless unknown men and women who have lived on these islands over the centuries. The same is true of folk Hinduism in India and popular Daoism in China. This point could reflect the major difference between Western and Eastern traditions, with the partial exception of Buddhism. The former is focused on individual accomplishment and the latter is organic and responds to subtle, underlying natural forces.

There is, however, a more positive aspect to Shinto's lack of a founder, which becomes clear as soon as we learn one of the first premises of Shinto, that "teaching does not come from human beings." Shinto is therefore defined as "a religion revering great nature." Our ancestors had a profound perception of the law of nature and the mysteries held within the natural world. They experienced a sense of awe and gratitude toward those mysteries and expressed this sensibility through myth and ritual. This is the essence of Shinto, and so we could say that Shinto's true founder is nature herself.

Shinto's perspective is that mystical experiences, revelations given to someone, or man-made philosophies are often fallible, precisely because they come from human beings. Therefore, we should not accord an unnecessary importance to them, and we should remember that they can at times become obstacles to spiritual development.

Shinto has no doctrines

Without a founder, Shinto is also without any systematic doctrine connected to a founder's teachings. Therefore, there are no dogmas, absolute codes, orders, nor laws applying to Shinto as a whole.

The *Kojiki* (the Ancient Chronicles of Japan) of 712 and the *Nihonshoki* (Chronicles of Japan) of 720, which have many Shinto themes, are not sacred texts akin to the Bible or the Koran. In the Japanese texts, historical facts, myths, and theology are harmoniously blended with political twists and literary embellishments. Therefore, we have to read and interpret them with full attention and care, because every word is not necessarily considered as sacred. Also, we should always be aware that books written by Shintoists do not attempt to set out doctrine for the whole of Shinto.

Although Shinto contains the ideas of purification, *kiyome*, and cleansing, *harai*,[6] these are not based on fixed doctrines. None of the sayings of Shinto thinkers, such as "revere Kami and respect ancestors" can be interpreted as doctrines. Further, the philosophy of one spirit, four souls (*ichirei shikon*; see Chapter 6) handed down in Yamakage Shinto is not a doctrine.

The late Dr. Jean Herbert, who taught at the University of Geneva in Switzerland, lived in Japan for a long time and studied Shinto deeply. I assisted him in his study for six years. At the presentation of his final report on Shinto, he said the following:

> "I met over one thousand Shinto priests and Shintoists, and I have never heard the same words from each of them. In Shinto, people don't talk in the same pattern. They neither need nor are obliged to talk in the same fashion."

For most Westerners this observation must surely be remarkable; for Christian believers anywhere in the world refer to the same body of teachings to explain their faith. Shinto, however, does not require such standardization of belief and practice. Shintoists observe great nature and speak about it from diverse viewpoints; therefore the philosophies they preach are of various kinds and not always in accord with each other. Yet this does not in itself matter, there are not many Shintoists who really want, or feel the need, to discuss doctrine at all, let alone engage in doctrinal disputes.

This is why it is often said that Shinto does not have a strong critical faculty. Shinto does not go in for wordy discussion for detail, which in practice means setting language on a pedestal, as if words were in themselves absolute.

As well as Shintoists, many Japanese generally don't believe in words very much. They understand that it is wrong to consider human language as absolute, recognizing that human existence is very small and limited when compared with the great nature. The Western mentality that treats human knowledge and language as absolutes is, from Shinto's perspective, a form of human arrogance.

No matter how hard one works to construct a theology with long strings of elaborate words, those words cannot contain either the world of great nature or the world of the spirit of Kami. In Shinto, it is important for each person to experience and feel in his or her own way and not to use language to force others to believe in a certain way.

Can we say that Shinto is one system, even though it doesn't have a unified teaching or view of the universe?

Dr. Herbert continued: "...when I linked everybody's sayings together, I can see one philosophy and one set of philosophical principles emerging. We cannot say, then, that Shinto is undeveloped."

If you look deeply into Shinto, you can find a philosophical core. It cannot be defined in only a few words, and it can be explained from more than one perspective. No explanation is absolute, but putting the different explanations together brings out the essence of Shinto philosophy.

One can also argue that religion does not exist solely or primarily at the level of language. This is why rituals and festivals are the great lifeline in Shinto, and they are far more than mere manners and customs. The wonderful teachings and views about life embedded in each of these ritual gestures and actions have been handed down throughout recorded history. Participants feel these and can have mystical experiences through their practices.

Many traditional festivals handed down in each geographical region express rich and subtle thoughts and a sense of awe toward Kami. These expressions take the form of actions and rituals, without the use of logic or language.

The mental attitude—as opposed to the words and sermons—of the priests who are deeply committed to the devout life can move many people's hearts. We cannot necessarily say that a priest is impious just because he cannot articulate much about the rites and manners he is performing.

In Shinto, the spiritual tradition is allowed to evolve freely, since there is no definite pattern or model. Because of this some Shinto ideas can certainly go off track. Philosophies explained by each Shintoist might bring out diverse levels of the tradition, some superior and some inferior. But in Shinto we do not criticize or eliminate them in the name of some absolute authority or power. This is probably because Shinto takes a far-sighted view that low-level or wrong ideas will eventually be naturally eliminated in the long run.

But however formless Shinto appears to be, there are some underlying principles that make up its essence. It is to these that I shall turn my attention in the remainder of this book.

Shinto has no precepts or commandments

Since there is no doctrine espoused in Shinto, there are no absolute precepts. Precepts are admonitions or commandments that usually take the form of prohibitions ("do not do such and such") or injunctions ("do such and such"). These are, of course, ethical rules and disciplines that range from village or tribal regulations to the laws of nations.

There are two kinds of precepts—one for members of the religious order, governing the lives of monks and nuns, the other for laymen and women. There are also precepts that affect everyday actions, such as the preparation of meals, and precepts that apply to specific situations or times, such as festivals or periods of fasting.

Judaism and Islam, for instance, give quite detailed prohibition guidelines and have elaborate prohibitions and injunctions, deviation from which is often viewed as an obstacle to salvation. These monotheistic religions contain a strong concept of salvation by submission to the judgment of God, viewing humanity as corrupted by original sin and having to seek salvation through divine grace. Hinduism and Buddhism are also religions of salvation, which tend to see the world, and humanity, as inherently flawed. Following precepts is part of a path toward salvation, which is identical to an escape from human constraints.

In Shinto, however, we do not have precepts that perform this function. Certainly we provide advice, such as the admonition cited above to revere Kami and respect ancestors, but this does not prescribe people's behavior in detail. There are also taboos in Shinto such as white uncleanness (pollution by death and funerals) and red uncleanness (pollution by blood and menstruation). There are also some other taboos for priests and those conducting rituals. These are limited only to special occasions of ritual services for Kami in which people seek to have contact with Kami. They are not concerned with ordinary life.

Here a distinctive Shinto trait comes to the fore: "Shinto teaches neither salvation nor sin."

Most of the world's religions have a clear concept of sin, which can be applied to the individual's actions, choices, and thoughts. At the same time, they have an equally clear concept of forgiveness, atonement, and absolution, and a process by which these can be attained. Shinto, by contrast, does not possess a clear definition of sin. There is no equivalent of the original sin of traditional Christian doctrine, which taints humanity as a whole and from which each individual must transcend through repentance. Nor is there the karmic principle of cause and effect, characteristic of Buddhism and the Hindu dharma, in which our present circumstances can be determined by our actions in previous lives, and the spiritual goal is to move beyond the cycle of birth, death, and rebirth. Shinto is a religion without guilt, which assumes the essential goodness of humanity and each individual's potential for good.

Although Shinto is free from notions of sin and guilt, it does have an awareness of good and evil that is at once simple and subtle. Shinto conceives of good and evil in aesthetic terms, likening them to straight and curved lines. To the Japanese sensibility, a straight line is inherently beautiful. It need not be rigidly straight, but its emphasis should be forward and positive, signifying organic growth, clarity, and honesty. A sacred tree, such as the cedar or cypress, has a straight outline and its branches reach toward the heavens. It is a coherent, organic structure, simple yet intricate, and without blemish.

The same principle is applied to Japanese craftsmanship, traditional and modern. In the design of buildings, in carpentry, painting, and needlework, there is an emphasis on the clear, simple line rather than unnecessary curves and complexities. In *ikebana*, the traditional Japanese art of flower arrangement, the straight and simple pattern is associated with nobility. The emphasis, as in all the Japanese decorative arts, is on understatement rather than exaggeration, and this principle is derived from the Shinto sensibility. In the practical arts, the same principle applies. The carpenter, for instance, often dedicates his inking string—by which he measures straight lines—to the Shinto shrine so that it assumes a sacred significance.

The *norito* includes the entreaty "please make it straight." Misfortune is associated with all that is warped, curved, or crooked, including one's own mind and heart. It is attributed to *magatsubi*, the curved spirit, that can be around us or within us. That curved spirit is the origin of our own evil deeds and any misfortunes or disasters. Evil deeds and thoughts arise from the operation of the curved spirit, because the imbalance it creates leads us away from that which is straight and clear. Shinto divides evil deeds into two categories—*amatsu tsumi*, the most pernicious crimes of all; and *kunitsu tsumi*, or more conventional misdemeanors. The sins belonging to the former category, *amatsu tsumi*, are described in the *Kojiki* and the *Nihonshoki* as the "raging victory of *Susanoo*" against his sister *Amaterasu*, and were actually offences destructive of agriculture. Distortion of the food-line is seen as a heavenly sin, while the earthly sins or *kunitsu tsumi* are seen as evil deeds committed by people who are possessed by spirits.

In the English language, the word "straight" is traditionally associated with honesty and clear thinking, whilst the words "crooked" or "twisted" are associated with dishonesty and neurosis. In Shinto, these concepts form the basis of moral judgment. Good or moral behavior is associated with balance of mind, body, and spirit; evil or immoral behavior with imbalance, be it spiritual, intellectual, or physical. In Shinto, ethics and aesthetics are closely entwined.

Shinto has no idols

Every religion has some objects of worship. It was common for people in the ancient worlds of Mesopotamia, Egypt, Greece, and Rome to create statues or carvings of their gods, saints, and holy men, and to worship them, or use them as instruments of worship known as icons. Judaism distinguished itself from these ancient religions by advocating the prohibition of idols. Christianity created images of Christ, the

Virgin Mary, and the Saints in order to help disseminate its teachings to the masses.

Buddhism originally did not involve the worship of images, but as it spread and absorbed a wide range of local traditions and practices, icons and idols of various kinds emerged. Initially, the sculpted depictions of the Buddha owed much to the influence of classical Greece. Ordinary people have a powerful need for icons and images as objects for prayer, and so the idol, in whatever form, inevitably becomes a precious, sacred object for them.

In Shinto, during a certain period in the medieval age when it was most strongly interacting with Buddhism, images of Kami were made, mostly at the level of folk religion. Yet it is safe to say that Shinto does not have any lasting or profound tradition of sculpted images or statues in human form. It is true that people make their ceremonies by facing the sanctuary of the shrine or the rock, which is called *iwakura*, or rock seat. This does not necessarily mean they are worshipping either the shrine or the rock itself, and that they treat them as icons. They are merely places where the worshiper finds spiritual inspiration and so journeys from one level of reality to another, experiencing a true connection with Kami.

How, then, should we interpret the mirror (*kagami*) put at the innermost part of the sanctuary? What is the mirror? This is a very difficult question to answer. The mirror is the precious treasure-like tool reflecting the image of Kami. It is also the symbol of the sun, the

Iwakura

source of all life and the symbol of spiritual light when spirit of Kami (*shinrei*) manifests itself in this world.[7] For some, *kagami* represents not the mirror but rather the *kagami*-shining look or the *kagami*-shining body. In either case, it is the bright, shining, radiant light body, reflecting the spirit of Kami but not representing Kami in a material form. It is an abstract symbol, and so we cannot say that it is an image or idol.

Kagami, mirror

The *hakuhei* (white paper cut and folded in special sacred forms) should also not be misinterpreted as an image or idol. *Hakuhei* is used for exorcism or purification, and it can be found at the front of the shrine. *Hakuhei* was originally used for a very precious offering to Kami and was later considered as *yorishiro* for Kami's presence. It has become the ritual tool for purifying people from *kegare* (impurity or uncleanness). We cannot consider the *hakuhei* as an image of Kami.

Some have alleged that Shinto has no idols because of the inferior

 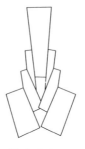 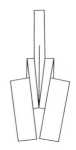

Hakuhei

skills of the Japanese in representational arts. I do not think that this is a correct view, because Japan has an artistic heritage that is as rich as any in the world! Instead of denigrating Japanese creativity, as too many people—including many Japanese—have tended to do, we should consider an alternative explanation. Whereas the West, and to a large extent the Indic traditions, seek a concrete image of God, identifiable with an individual physical body, the Japanese are quite free from such constraints. They see no need to mould the divine in human form in order to recognize it.

Both form and body are seen as temporary and transient by the Japanese. This notion is intimately connected to the spirit of Shinto. As we shall see in the next chapter, even the shrine did not exist in Shinto's original form.

Shinto has no organization

In early Shinto, not only was there no shrine building but there was also no central organization. Although each village had an organization for each festival for Kami, and each powerful shrine had an organization for its rituals, they each still acted as an independent entity. Therefore, we can say that there was no Shinto organization at either a social or national level. This means that there was neither a central organization nor a unified religious body.

In the medieval age, Yoshida Shinto appeared in Shinto history and established the license system to counter Buddhism. Through the Shirakawa priest lineage family, established earlier than Yoshida Shinto, licenses were issued to counter Yoshida Shinto. There was no organization, however, either to bring the various shrines together for the training and deployment of priests, or to create a unified structure for Shinto.

Therefore, it was an unprecedented situation for Shinto to be faced with government control in the beginning of the Meiji Era in 1868. Later, following Japan's defeat in World War II, so-called "National" or "State" Shinto was eliminated. After 1945 the voluntarily united shrines group (*Jinja honcho*) remained, with a central headquarters. There are still many shrines and Shinto sects outside of this group.

The tragedy of "not-having-any"

Shinto, then, has no founder, no doctrine, no commandments, no idols, and no organization. What it does have are ambiguous characteristics like sympathy and silent experience. This is the very reason why it has been often considered a non-religion by Japanese scholars as well as foreign intellectuals. Japan's unique historical circumstances and cultural background explain the development of Shinto at the intuitive rather than overtly intellectual level.

Japan is surrounded in every direction by sea, and it has kept relative peace with its neighbors for much of its history, the aberrations of the twentieth century notwithstanding. Japan suffered no major invasions or mass emigrations, despite some incursions and considerable cultural influences from Korea and China. Throughout her history, Japan has remained a remarkably homogeneous nation and I believe that this explains many of the characteristics of Shinto, and of Japanese culture more generally. In particular, the characteristic of not pursuing any theory or system is explained by this historical fact. In a homogeneous society, there is less competition between ideas or schools of thought.

But this uniformity turned out to be a significant weakness when Japan was brought face to face with other civilizations and ways of life. After the Meiji Restoration in 1868 and then World War II, Western civilization engulfed Japan and suppressed many of its traditional values and instincts.

Let us consider further the cultural flood from the west. Since the so-called "Cultural Enlightenment" of the Meiji era, "Culture" has largely meant "Western culture." Culture belongs to the West, and being intellectual generally means being someone who imports Western culture to Japan. Models of culture are in the West, so people who love the traditional Japanese culture without knowledge of Western culture are considered anachronistic and bigoted. Yuurei Mori, Secretary of Education in the Meiji Government, who was an admirer of the West, once famously used his walking stick to lift the white silk veil that protects the Ise shrine from the view of visitors. This incident neatly symbolized the state of the Japanese nation in the Meiji era.

During this time of great turmoil, Shinto was forced to mutate into a distorted, nationalized religion, of which grotesque ethnocentrism was the most notable characteristic. We could say that this ethnocentrism was the result of the reaction to admiration of the West. Shinto, lacking its own solid doctrine and theory, ended up revealing this weakness. Then after the country's defeat in World War II, when nationalized Shinto was destroyed, Shinto went into decline.

During this tumultuous time there was certainly a handful of people trying to re-establish the essence of Shinto and appeal to society with the practice of the faith. However, it was a weak and small movement facing a trend that was consuming the whole of society.

Japanese atheists and faithless Japanese

In this way, a peculiar form of society was created in Japan after World War II. The birth of such a secular, materialistic, and atheistic society perhaps cannot be found in any other age and place in history.

It is said that most Japanese, when asked for their religious status in filling out an application form for a passport or questionnaire, will answer "none." When the Japanese adopted only the materialistic and abstract parts of Western civilization, they equated atheism, or at least the absence of faith, with rationalism, humanism, and becoming a fully "civilized" people.

We can say that the great influx of atheism and materialism into Japan had a serious influence on the Japanese mind, where the notion of Kami and spirit-soul (*reikon*) are increasingly disappearing. Human beings are seen as simply material things, and there is no concept of an afterlife or a sense of continuity in the dominant culture of modern Japan. This view of the world has steadily undermined rather than enhanced the humanist conceptions of freedom, responsibility, and dignity. When human beings become conscious of an afterlife, of a higher being or beings, or of the possibility of rebirth, they are more likely to think beyond their immediate material interests. But when assuming everything is finished with death, people might conclude that they can do anything as long as they are not violating man-made laws—or as long as they are managing to escape punishment. Then their absolute goals are satisfying their short-term desires and the prolongation of life at all costs. Ultimately, such questions as "what does it really mean to be human?" or "what values should human beings pursue?" begin to disappear.

However there is much evidence that, in Japan and in the West, the pendulum is starting to swing the other way. As the social and environmental costs of materialism become more apparent, people are inclined once again to ask deeper questions. They have recently started feeling a strong desire for pursuing meaning, values, and ethics. This is clearly manifested in the recent booming interest in mysticism known as the New Age movement and the events created by the new occult religions. There is a serious danger that, in a climate of spiritual ignorance, such movements can assume a distorted or perverse form. In the Japanese context, the most extreme example of this tendency is the AUM group, whose members released poisoned gas on the Tokyo subway in 1995. The existence of occult movements, however extreme or grotesque, should be seen as evidence of a spiritual crisis, just as when extremist political movements (including terrorist groups) emerge, it is an indication of social malaise. In Japan, as elsewhere, there are millions of spiritually hungry people who are searching for explanations beyond the purely material.

At the same time, established religious organizations are losing their spiritual influence and ability to respond to widespread spiritual hunger. It is because they tend merely to reflect modernity rather than engage critically with the modern world. The more abstract and "intellectual" they become, the more they become materialistic and worldly, and so lose their spiritual dimension. Therefore, with few choices left, people are readily led into the dangerous occult world. Many of the new occult religious groups cynically distort the inner teachings of the traditional religions. They give, or more often sell, instant spiritual teachings to anyone who requests them, whether or not they are truly open to or ready for spiritual advancement. This can have harmful and destabilizing effects on the individuals concerned and even on the teachings themselves.

When human beings develop their innate and mysterious powers, such as miraculous healing gifts or supernatural abilities like clairvoyance, they need to display in their work a sensitivity toward human nature in all its aspects, as well as an understanding of the balance between humanity and the natural world. This is the ethos that should govern psychic abilities if they are to have beneficial rather than harmful effects.

Not only Shinto but also any religion with a long tradition knows this very well and has the methods to convey its esoteric aspects. But in the new religions, people are easily excited by occasional flashes of psychic inspiration. They are not encouraged to explore such powers with caution, as rare and special gifts that can inflict great harm as well as accomplish immense good. The result of spiritual impetuosity is the collective hysteria associated with the occult.

Characteristics of Shinto

Shinto is often referred to as polytheistic, because there are many Kami. In the *norito*, Kami are classified in three ways: *amatsukami* (heavenly Kami), *kunitsukami* (earthly Kami) and *yaoyorozu no kami* (myriad other Kami). Kami are therefore not necessarily deities in the sense that is usually understood, but possess a wide variety of spiritual powers and attributes. Shinto can therefore be described as polytheistic in the context of its *amatsukami*, who correspond most closely to the idea of "gods." However, it is also important to remember that *all* Kami are interconnected and spring from a single source—the essence of Shinto. Kami are both many and one, both individual entities and parts of a whole. The three categories of Kami described by the *norito* are not rigidly divided, but interact and overlap. Therefore the term "polytheism" is far from a full definition of Shinto. It is only partially descriptive, and is useful only when it helps us to understand that Shinto is a path of peaceful coexistence, in which each person's beliefs and experiences are valued. It does not matter how one believes in and chooses to describe the divine power or powers, as long as that belief is not used to justify destructive ambitions, or to do evil to others.

Another point is that Shinto neither excludes mystical abilities nor praises them excessively. If a person is a Shintoist, he or she knows very well the fact that various kinds of mysterious phenomena occur. He or she also knows the dangers that can arise through mystical experience, and how such experiences should be handled.

Some argue that Shinto is profane, but this displays a misunderstanding of its nature and essential characteristics. I certainly understand that Buddhism interprets this worldly existence as suffering, so it has a strong tendency to seek salvation in the other world. Shinto, by contrast, is at its core a life-affirming faith. Living in the world is a positive experience, but it is not regarded as the only reality and never should the presence and power of an "unseen" world be denied.

Shinto values nature and life. This is because Shinto originally arose from a sense of gratitude and awe toward great nature. Our ancestors loved nature, from animals and plants to mountains and rivers. This love of nature is intrinsic to the Japanese character, influencing our art forms as well as our spiritual practices, even in a modern, urbanized nation where millions of people have little apparent contact with nature. In this age when human beings are destroying mother earth in the pursuit of material progress, we should reclaim our love for nature and let it inform our daily lives and spiritual practices.

Shinto is, ultimately, such a simple belief that anybody can accept and practice it. It neither requires special intellectual ability nor does it demand a life-denying asceticism. As long as people understand the attitudes associated with cleanness and brightness (happiness) and rightness and straightness (honesty),[8] they can start from those points and advance further along the path to explore more profound themes. One of the strengths of Shinto is that it can allow people to find their own level of practice and experience, without being physically or intellectually overwhelmed, but gaining as much spiritual awareness as practitioners of more stringent or austere paths.

What is *koshinto* (ancient Shinto)?

Most of the themes of this book are taken from Yamakage Shinto, which was handed down through the Yamakage family for many generations. The author of this book is the 79th successor. Yamakage Shinto is also known as *koshinto*.

Since the purpose of this book is not the presentation of Shinto history, I shall not dwell on this. It is worth remembering, however, that Shinto has evolved and radically altered through the ages. The Shinto line as we understand it today begins in the era before Buddhism arrived in Japan. Then, with the arrival and influence of Buddhism, Shugo Shinto was born. "Shugo" literally means "learned and integrated Shinto." This uniquely Japanese religion was born out of the interaction and overlap between Shinto and Buddhism. Then Yoshida Shinto developed, which integrated the way of yin and yang inherited from Daoist influences. Later, Shirakawa Shinto and Great Shrine Family Shinto (*Shake* Shinto) developed. This line was traditionally handed down to a priest family of a Great Shrine (*Taisha*) such as the shrines at Ise, Kamo, Izumo, Usa, or Munakata. National Shinto evolved after the Meiji Restoration, and most recently the organized system of *Jinja* Shinto (meaning Shrine Shinto) was established after World War II.

When we exclude both the Shinto traditions of the medieval age, which have strong Buddhist influences, and then the modern-era Shinto from all those lines mentioned above, then what remains is the so-called *koshinto*. This has been handed down to a few families and

Shinto lines and has so been preserved since antiquity. There are also some more modern *koshinto* groups that were established by independent practitioners of Shinto during the Meiji era and the Edo period before it. They collected old traditions and legends and put them together into spiritual systems.

In *koshinto*, the systematic methods of exercise and training are important. There are several lines of *koshinto*, of which only a very few are orthodox. The systematic methods that Yamakage Shinto teaches are orthodox lines, so that when a person masters this method, that person gains not only mystical ability but also a deep and all-encompassing knowledge of the universe. Nowadays, many people want one real experience instead of detailed words explaining the doctrine. There are many lines of *koshinto* that do not make their knowledge available to the general public, because they regard it as esoteric. But Yamakage Shinto aims at transmitting the right methods to as many people as possible by opening to them the gates of knowledge.

The Yamakage is a trusted *koshinto* family, serving successive emperors. Tanba no Ason Yasunori, who wrote the oldest medical book in Japan, *The Method of Heart of Medicine*, is the 47th in the Yamakage line of succession. The 75th successor, Yamakage Kazuhira (1751–1810) is the eldest son and heir of the Vice Greatest High Priest in the second rank Hagiwara Kazumiki, who is from a branch family of Yoshida Shinto. While using the hereditary esoteric knowledge as a base, this 75th successor added Yoshida Shinto, Suika Shinto, and aspects of other schools to ancient *koshinto* and integrated them to create the foundation of Yamakage Shinto. The 76th successor, Nakayama Tadakore (1804–64), is an illegitimate son of the Emperor Kokaku, and he committed suicide at Settsu during his involvement in the overthrow of the Shogunate. Nakayama Tadahide (1846–1916) succeeded him, and then came the 78th successor, Nakayama Tadanori. Presently, I am the 79th successor.

Of course our Yamakage Shinto has also been strongly colored by the influences of Buddhism, Confucianism, and Daoism. However, it encapsulates the pure and ancient Shinto tradition, the light of which radiates from it. It contains hidden views of the universe, nature, and spirit-soul.

In the next chapter I shall begin to explain the world of Yamakage Shinto.

CHAPTER 3

What is *Jinja*?

No need for a "building"

In Shinto, the term *jinja* is used for a shrine, or more literally the dwelling place of Kami. Many people probably have a mental picture of a building whenever they think of a Shinto shrine. It is said that we now have 80,000 such buildings in Japan, of which 6,000 have resident *kannushi* (Shinto masters). Out of these, 280 shrines are famous and called *kanpei-sha*. These are shrines with a high status because of their relation with upper class families, including the emperor's. There are also *kokuhei-sha* shrines, which mean shrines supported by local governments.

When foreigners first visit Japan, they often find it hard to tell the difference between Shinto shrines and Buddhist temples. Nowadays a growing number of young Japanese also seem to be unable to tell the difference. It is true that we have only a few remaining elements in a shrine which are unique to Shinto and show obvious differences with Buddhism—for example, marks or symbols such as the *torii* (gate), *shimenawa* (plaited straw rope to protect the shrine), a sacred mirror, and *hakuhei* (paper cut in a particular form). But there are sometimes Buddhist temples that also include a shrine for a tutelary deity or a guardian deity as well as the typical Buddhist iconography. This creates even

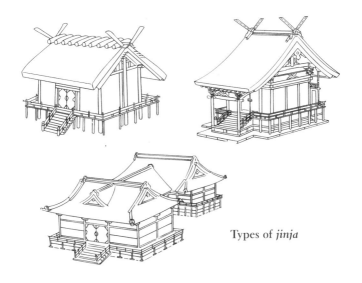

Types of *jinja*

more confusion for some people. There are also various styles of shrine buildings, some of which do not have a *chigi* or a *katsuogi*, which are usually distinguishing features of a Shinto shrine.

There are good reasons for this seemingly strange state of affairs. To begin with, shrines were built in imitation of the early Japanese Buddhists, who began constructing temples. Then, during the middle ages, Buddhist ideas gradually blended with the way of Kami, and so their rituals acquired similar characteristics. Originally, however, Shinto did not have a building or mirror to mark the sacred area.

In the present Shinto practice, a building is used for worship in which is placed a symbolic object called *goshintai*. The literal meaning of *goshintai* is "the body of Kami." It is a material object representing the spirit of Kami (*shinrei*). Like a body it contains the spirit of Kami when it comes down to manifest its presence in this world. Buildings containing *goshintai* are considered as places where Kami reside. In the original Shinto tradition, however, Kami neither reside permanently in buildings nor in *goshintai*. In the past, at the proper time, people created a proper sacred place, celebrated and worshipped there, and welcomed the spirit of Kami.

Kannabi, iwasaka, himorogi

We refer to the place where people welcome the spirit of Kami as *yuniwa*, literally meaning "purified yard or court." A special place suitable for this *yuniwa* is called *kannabi*, and the center where the spirit of Kami comes down to be present there is called *itsu no iwasaka*. This means a sacred enclosure with a rock at the center.

Traditional practice also involved the planting or temporary positioning of a *sakaki* tree at the center of the sacred space to mark the *itsu no iwasaka*. The *sakaki* is a small evergreen with shiny leaves indigenous to Japan. It acted as an invocation of the spirit of Kami. Trees used for ritual purposes are known as *himorogi*.

Himorogi functions as a *yorishiro* for the spirit of Kami. *Yorishiro* is a spiritual antenna for the spirit of Kami to descend in order to manifest its presence. There are several types of *yorishiro*, including trees, stones, rocks, or in some cases animals.

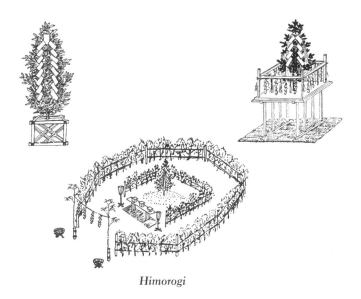

Himorogi

These words, *himorogi* and *iwasaka*, are ancient terms that can be found in the Chronicles of Japan (*Nihonshoki*) of 720, in the section that describes the arrival on earth of the descendants of the sun-goddess. Sometimes the written characters for *himorogi* are pronounced as *kamigaki*, which literally means "Kami's fence" or "sacred fence." In this case it means the whole of the *yuniwa*, that is to say the purified or sacred space where the presence of Kami can be felt.

Somewhat later, people began hooking *hakuhei* (paper cut in a special way), hemp material, a mirror, or other objects on the branch of the *himorogi*. At purification ceremonies for building sites, when the corner stone is laid, people still now purify the area by enclosing it with a plaited straw rope (*shimenawa*), putting up *himorogi*, and welcoming the spirit of Kami. This is also a form of *yuniwa* and people originally celebrated and worshipped the spirit of Kami by creating *yuniwa* in this way at each festival. When they finished the ceremony, they removed the sacred area. This is the traditional way, rather than the use of buildings designated exclusively for Shinto practice.

Our ancestors perceived the existence of special sacred places where festivals in honor of Kami could be held. Many of these special places, known as *kannabi*, were beautifully shaped mountains. The great shrines formerly connected with noble families, including the emperor's family, generally have a mountain behind them, and it is there that they put the inner shrine, or *okumiya*. This is a shrine situated in the courtyard at the back of the main shrine building, and dedicated to the same Kami. The reason for the existence of an inner shrine is that originally the *kannabi* mountain itself was the center for welcoming Kami. It was later replaced by a building for the use of worshipers.

Typical examples of *kannabi* are found at Omiwa Jinja in Nara prefecture, Munakata Taisha in Fukuoka prefecture, Kamigamo Jinja in Kyoto, Kasuga Taisha in Nara, and Asama Taisha at Mt. Fuji. Omiwa Jinja, which is understood to be dedicated to Miwa Myojin, has no inner shrine building even at this time. Mt. Miwa itself is defined as the body of Kami, or as the *goshintai*, the vessel for the spirit of Kami.

Sometimes a shrine was built at a different place from the *kannabi* where practice had traditionally taken place. Then, practitioners would travel to the original *kannabi* only when a festival was taking place. We call this kind of *kannabi otabisho*, which means the "place we travel to." One of the examples of this is the Iwakura Shrine in Kyoto. This type of "*kannabi* mountain" consists mostly of a huge rock, and people consider this to be a special place where the spirit of Kami descends to make its presence felt. This rock is called *iwakura*, or rock seat. A typical example is the huge rock of Mt. Kamikura in Kumano. There is also another type of *iwakura* that is made of several huge assembled rocks at the top of a mountain.

In Okinawa, the traditional, naturalistic forms of *kannabi* and *iwakura* have been left intact. There, people say *ibi* or *ibe* for *iwasaka*. A place of *kannabi* suitable for *iwasaka* is called *utaki*. This *utaki* is usually a huge rock or a rock mountain but can sometimes be a deep forest. The most famous ones are *Seifa utaki* (purified place of *utaki*) and *Sumuchina utaki*. The latter is located at the north part of the mainland of Okinawa. There is an incense burner there and the sacred space is open to devotees. This sacred space is known as *utoshi*, meaning "the entrance," or place to send a prayer. There they offer prayer to *nirai-kanai*, which can be translated literally as the "world of roots," or the "world of the source of all life," where Kami is enshrined.

The mystery of *iwakura*—rock seat

Oyamatsumi Jinja is located at Okuta in Kitakyushu city. Soon after

World War II, I became acquainted with the *kannushi* there and learned many interesting things from him. According to the *kannushi*, this particular Shrine had only *iwakura* even after the war, and sacred trees (*goshinboku*) were still thriving on the site. But before long, those trees had been cut down, and a shrine building was erected at the plateau in front of the place where we were standing. While listening to him, I recognized that this shrine was blessed with an ancient history, which was worth exploring at a more profound level.

At that time, I had a visionary dream that showed a bamboo thicket at the mountain behind the shrine, and *iwakura* shown beside a bamboo thicket. On the *iwakura*, there was a spherical light shining like the sun. Somewhat astonished, I described this to the *kannushi* the next morning and he said, "Yes, there is certainly a bamboo thicket there, but no such a thing as *iwakura*. But since it is a mountain, of course, we will find some rocks."

I decided to climb the mountain immediately. As I expected, I found *iwakura* under the thickly growing weeds. I did not know from which place these rocks had been brought, but in any case I found that several standing rocks were placed next to each other to form a ring. At the center of this ring, a large rock was sunk into the earth, as if it had sunk roots there. When I mentioned this to the *kannushi*, he decided to cut the surrounding weed. Several gardeners were brought to cut the weeds and ended up finding the clear shape of the *iwakura*. It was evening and the sun was setting. The *kannushi* then saw the *iwakura* lit up in red with the rays of the setting sun shining through the leaves of the trees from the west. At this, he sat down in awe. Then he described the new shrine building as a form of sacrilege and, expressing gratitude to Kami, also asked to be forgiven for his lack of knowledge. He told me that he felt as if he was returning to the sacred place of an ancient faith, in other words, to his spiritual roots.

Shortly afterward, he performed a ritual ceremony for welcoming Kami, choosing the date of the ceremony through divination. The chosen day was dark, with thick clouds in the sky. The place of *iwakura* appeared to be shrouded in twilight. When the rite of Kami's descent was finished, however, and at exactly the moment when the *keihitsu*[9] was uttered, a cloud suddenly cleared from one spot of the sky and the sunlight, like a spotlight, shone on the *iwakura*.

When he explained this to me through the telephone, his voice was trembling:

> "Master, it is truly awe-inspiring. This was really the place where the rays of the sunrise and also the sunset fell. I feel extremely grateful to know that this is the place where our ancestors welcomed Kami and celebrated in the distant past."

Shrines such as this Oyamatsumi Jinja, where the *iwakura* shines with direct rays from the sun at both sunrise and sunset, are survivors of the most ancient and authentic form of Shinto. We have such an *iwakura* at the top of Mount Omiwa in Nara. It is also often the case that there flows a special spiritual energy from this kind of *iwakura*. When you hold your hands close to the *iwakura*, you can feel something akin to a magnetic wave piercing your hands like a needle. Even after people have stopped performing rituals for *iwakura* at these sites, if it was not really influenced by unclean human energy and was rarely visited, then one can still feel a strong magnetic energy. Even if it was made unclean by humans, if the site has been well preserved from ancient times, one can still feel the energy when holding one's hands over it and praying sincerely in one's mind. People who are trained spiritually to a certain degree, or who have special abilities can easily sense this energy. Generally speaking, women, particularly young women, seem to possess a particular sensitivity.

In Okinawa, women with psychic powers or spiritual sensitivity are known as *noro* (priestess) or *yuta* (psychic medium). Among the *yuta*, there are sometimes people who suddenly manifest psychic or spiritual sensitivity only when they are older. They go to *utaki* for worship and they feel the spirit of Kami descending upon that site.

After the spirit of Kami descends a place becomes *jinja*

For a *jinja*, one must choose a suitable place and then create an appropriate setting for a sacred space. Then it is necessary to ask Kami to descend upon it and make its presence felt. In other words, *jinja* need not be a place where Kami have dwelled eternally, or will always live.

We call the shrine *kamigaki* or *kamiyashiro*. Both words mean the place where Kami stays. But *yashiro* means "temporal house." This usage of *shiro* can be seen in the word *katashiro*. *Kata* means "form" and *shiro* means "substitute—temporarily taking a role for an original one." Therefore *katashiro* is usually the representation of a real object or natural formation, taken as a symbolic substitute for temporary usage. This entire concept implies the ancient peoples' belief that the place where the spirit of Kami resides is in the much higher world of Kami, so even if we build a magnificent shrine on earth, it can only be a temporary one.

When I visited Okinawa, I was able to meet Kana Nakaizumi, the island's chief *noro*. She took me to the east coast beach, where I asked, "*noro*, where is *utaki*?" She held up her arms and pointed at the sky. "Look! It is there," she said. I looked to find a beautifully pure blue sky and a pure blue ocean. Truly, it was the boundless shrine for Kami with the sky as a celestial roof.

The ancients believed that it did not matter if a shrine were small and simple, because there is a huge shrine much higher in the world of the spirit of Kami where many Kami (*kamigami*) reside. This ancient belief underlies Shinto, as every *kannushi* serving at old shrines with a pious attitude might acknowledge. The same can be said for the shrine festivals. Various shrines have a festive ritual called *kanmizosai* (Kami's cloth festival). On these occasions, they dedicate clothing to Kami—mostly in the form of a miniature cloth. This is nothing but a *katashiro*, an object made as a temporary representation for the underlying spiritual reality, and so the size of the cloth is not relevant.

There is a mysterious belief that if our sincerity and prayer is contained in a *katashiro*, then it can be transformed into a great offering in the world of Kami.

It is also said that the Kami itself does not reside in the shrine. Rather, the guardian spirit is said to reside there. The guardian spirit protects *kamizane*, which literally means "Kami's core," acting as a substitute or *katashiro* for Kami. This guardian spirit is active in the world of spirit (*reikai*), which is at a lower level than the world of Kami (*shinkai*).[10] The role of this guardian spirit is to connect this earthly world with the higher world of Kami. We are told that when believers practice morning and evening worship, this guardian spirit from the world of spirit worships the great Kami in the world of Kami in order to convey the believers' prayers.

The proper attitude of mind for welcoming Kami

We have seen, then, that it is necessary first to choose carefully an appropriate place and arrange it in a way that enables it to become receptive to Kami. But that is not enough. More important than anything else is to approach the task with great care and with a deep and open-hearted sincerity. The person best equipped to perform this function is the *kannushi*.

In Shinto, the *kannushi* certainly must have a special knowledge of the proper way to approach Kami and how to address them. It is not enough, however, for a *kannushi* to simply be a scholar. If he is to be truly able to welcome Kami, and to serve as a conduit between Kami and the people, he needs to be thinking and acting in good faith—for good faith, and purity of heart, are the most important qualities of all in Shinto. Unfortunately, the faith of many *kannushi* nowadays seems questionable to me, even though they have graduated from Shinto college and have an abundance of scholarly information. To begin with, their learning itself tends to over-emphasize the modern trend toward rationalism. It excludes faith as well as anything connected with mystery. No matter how much information you absorb or how many facts you memorize, such bookish learning cannot automatically give you faith. Often, it simply clutters the brain without increasing spiritual sensitivity. No matter how hard a *kannushi* tries to communicate with Kami, if he cannot truly feel the presence of Kami in his heart, then the spirit of Kami does not descend.

As for the proper attitude for welcoming Kami, it is vital for the *kannushi* to have a reverential attitude with a feeling of awe and to prostrate himself in front of Kami. This reverential attitude, combined with a feeling of awe, can probably be described in the broadest sense as "an apologetic attitude." The *kannushi* must have an awe-inspired and humble attitude, which will make him feel like saying, "I am not worthy of evoking Kami and of being in front of the presence. I have much pollution within me and I am an unclean person. I beg forgiveness from the bottom of my heart and pray you will purify me."

To give deeper meaning to this attitude, we need correct behavior and manners. A *kannushi* must therefore carefully practice the conduct of his ritual services. To conduct his rituals in the proper manner, it is not enough for him merely to stick restrictively to the public service regulations for the job specification of *kannushi*. There are some *kannushi* who skip over offerings for Kami with indifference. This approach undermines the attitude of open-mindedness and modesty.

With each movement of the body one must contain and reflect reverence and respect toward Kami. If people deepen this reverential attitude, then not only by the way they carry the body but also by the integrity of their daily character will they naturally reveal their cleanness and brightness[11] and humility. Being around that person, others will be able to appreciate the outer and inner qualities—which we often call fragrance—worthy of one who serves Kami. I know many *kannushi* who are men and women of such noble character. When a *kannushi* of this caliber holds a ritual ceremony at his shrine, the service reaches a true level of solemnity. We feel awe-struck in front of the shrine and we feel that Kami is truly present. A refreshing sense of tranquility pervades such shrines, and a spirit of benign humility is transmitted from older to younger generations of *kannushi*. In fact, the *kannushi*, serving in a shrine, should be sincere, otherwise the act of reverence cannot become truly pure, and the shrine cannot become a suitable *yuniwa*. Therefore, whether or not the spirit of Kami descends to the festival site depends upon how well the *kannushi* cultivates his moral character on a daily basis.

It is indeed like Hakuseki Arai says: "The power of the divine light increases by receiving human reverence." Spiritual energy will not be enhanced at the site of the shrine, and the light of Kami spirit will not permeate there until people pray to Kami with profound and sincere reverence.

One day, after listening to my interpretation of Shinto, a *kannushi* said this:

"Shrines should gather parishioners together and not teach them, I believe. We should not give any lectures to those who come to pay respect at the shrine or to visit the office of the shrine. We have to respect their positions or ideas. We should neither criticize them nor force them to follow our ideas. For the shrine is the public facility, and we don't ask which religion or sect they belong to. The shrine is not the place we give moral education. It is the place where they freely feel and learn something in their own way. Therefore, I devote myself with my whole heart to clean the place of the shrine, and I think it will satisfy me if people feel the spirit of Kami or learn some morality in their own way by immersing themselves in the clean atmosphere of the shrine."

This *kannushi* was conveying some sense of what a shrine ought to mean, to *kannushi* and visitors alike. For the purpose of a shrine is not to impose a single idea or belief system, but to create a pervasive sense of reverence and awe and so enable us to access the spiritual dimension.

Why *jinja* avoids *kegare* (impurity or uncleanness)

The body of Kami called *katashiro* is usually represented by the mirror, but this mirror itself is not Kami. When a mirror is put in the right place and is revered, the spirit of Kami descends upon the mirror, through which its spiritual vibration permeates the surrounding area. Only then does the mirror become *kamizane*. And if the spirit of Kami always visits this site, only then does it become the shrine where Kami is present.

In order for this to happen, the body of Kami and the place dedicated to it must be very clean and pure. Some people cannot understand this, and say, "The spirit of Kami has a great power of purification. It will clean itself even when the ceremonial service site and the body of Kami, such as a mirror, are impure." This idea is wrong.

The body of Kami is often enveloped and folded many times and put in the clean box. It is then enshrined in the *kamidoko* (Kami's floor), which is called *naijin*, the sanctuary of the main shrine. This *naijin* is surrounded by its outer enclosure called *gejin*. This *gejin* is the inner wall of the main shrine and is made of wood. The main shrine is also surrounded with another outer enclosure, which is in turn surrounded by fences—first the *mizugaki* then the *uchitamagaki* and finally the *sototamagaki*. The inside of these areas are called *kinsokuchi*, meaning "an area not allowed for feet to step on." People are prohibited from entering there.

Why is the cleanness of the shrine protected many times over? The body of Kami and the place for the descent of the spirit of Kami are still of physical matter itself, and matter can be easily contaminated.

Therefore, we work hard to keep the whole of the sacred space clean and pure.

When the sacred area is contaminated, the spiritual vibration of the spirit of Kami cannot permeate. This is because the spiritual light is cut off, in much the same way that a dirty, clouded mirror does not reflect objects well. The spirit of Kami does not clean the impurity by itself. It simply turns off the source switch of spiritual vibration and light.

As referred to above, what is enshrined is not Kami itself but rather the guardian spirit guarding *kamizane* (such as a mirror), which is actually *katashiro* for Kami, an object temporarily representing Kami. This guardian spirit also leaves unclean places and avoids humans who are not respectful.

Opening the path to Kami

In Yamakage Shinto, before prayers are to be offered to Kami, the sanctuary enshrining the body of Kami is first purified with *harainusa*.

This is the purification tool that was made of linen or hemp cloth in early times and was later made of paper. After purifying the sanctuary, the offerings of food and the *tamagushi* (a sprig of the sacred tree), the visitors and participants are finally purified. Students who have studied at a common Shinto university will likely be surprised at this scene. This is because only offerings and visitors are usually purified, not the sanctuary.

However, in order to request the spirit of Kami to descend and manifest its presence, *kamizane* as *yorishiro* has to be purified. We touched

Kannusa, or *harainusa*

on the *yorishiro* at the start of this chapter. It is a word used to describe a material object for Kami to descend upon in order to be present. *Yori* means the base for dwelling; therefore *yorishiro* is a worldly base, a temporary container of Kami. It is therefore essential to cleanse the sanctuary. But above all, we first have to purify our own prayer's path. In Yamakage Shinto, we call this "opening the path to Kami."

In order to open the path through which the spiritual wave of Kami's spirit can pass, we first cleanse the path, the *kamizane* (*yorishiro*), and the visitors. Only when everything and everybody involved is purified can humans possibly come in contact with the spirit of Kami.

It is generally accepted that the main shrine is where Kami resides, and so it requires no cleaning by the *kannushi* as it is inherently clean. But this idea is wrong because the main shrine is not the place where Kami always resides, even though it is the place where the power of the spirit of Kami can be contained. For this reason, we must purify the place. The purification for the main shrine must be done daily as well as at each ceremony.

The domain for the lower-level spirits

The spirit of Kami does not visit unclean places, and an unclean shrine becomes a mere building devoid of Kami energy, even though it may still have *mitamashiro* there. *Mitamashiro* is a material object temporarily representing spirit, such as a mirror, for the spirit of Kami to descend upon. Nowadays, in Shinto society, many *kannushi* are unaware of this impurity and its truly dreadful significance. It is a sad fact, therefore, that a growing number of shrines are without the presence of the spirit of Kami.

Even the status of national treasure that may be granted to a shrine does not necessarily guarantee the presence of the noble spirit of Kami. In modern Japan, a site is designated a national treasure or important cultural property purely because of the character of the building, and without any necessary relationship to the presence of the spirit of Kami. In some shrine buildings, when *kannushi* of low spiritual levels are serving, one can sense the presence of shady, lower-level spirits. These correspond to the *kannushi*'s own level of spiritual development. It often happens that only malevolent spirits, not good spirits, gather at places where large sums of money are demanded from visitors. Often, this happens with newly established religious groups. When people go to such places, they experience headaches or nausea.

One day I had an opportunity to visit a certain shrine and was invited to climb to the inner shrine by a fellow visitor. It was a mountain about 500 meters high above sea level, but it was still quite rugged. At the middle section of the path, there was a little Myoken Temple, named after the Myoken Bodhisattva. This name is a relic of the era when Kami and Buddha were merged. Many people from neighboring areas came to worship there, and the shrine was a thriving place before the war. But it is now dilapidated and crumbling. The roof is falling in, and the temple itself is damaged. It is more reminiscent of a haunted house than a shrine.

I passed the building and climbed toward the summit. Not long afterwards, I started feeling faint, as if there were some heaviness in my head. I wondered if I might not be in good shape as it had been a long time since my last climb. I went to the summit shrine and worshipped there, but experienced no significant Kami energy there at all.

"Master, does the noble spirit of Kami descend to be present here at this inner shrine?" asked my hiking companion. I replied: "Since my spiritual sensitivity has not been sharp these days, I probably can't tell very well, but I don't think we can say this place is a clean spiritual place. Indeed it is a place that has been made unclean. The spirit of Kami can't descend in such a place."

We went down the mountain and took our leave of the shrine. On the way to Hamamatsu in the car I felt very sluggish and heavy in the calves of my legs, as if they had gone to sleep. Some spirit at a lower level than my guardian spirit had possessed and responded to me. After I discerned the identity of this low-level spirit, I found that it was the spirit who had been residing at the Myoken Temple. And so I changed my vibration, prayed to my guardian spirit of Kami, and the leg immediately recovered. With the heaviness of the leg gone I was even able to take a nap. When we arrived at Kireigu—the main shrine of Yamakage Shinto—and went to each shrine to pay our respects, I heard a young person cry out, "Ow! I have such a headache! Where did that come from?" The ghostly aura of that low-level spirit was still inside the car.

Thus even a shrine known as a sacred place in the past can become the domain for malevolent spirits if people no longer offer prayers or take the time and care to keep it clean.

What is the household shrine (*kamidana*)?

The *kamidana*, household altar, can be considered a little shrine welcoming the spirit of Kami. Therefore, if we set it up in an appropriate place and in an appropriate way, carefully keep it clean, and offer prayers with a revering heart and mind, then the light of the noble spirit of Kami will permeate there.

In order to make a proper household shrine, we must put *kamizane* and other things there with a proper, formal procedure. There are several ways to install the shrine. The following guidelines apply:

1) It can be set up at a high position.

2) It can be at a floor level that has three or four steps. This is called "the Floor for Kami" (*kamidoko*).

3) It can be kept in a special niche (*tokonoma*) with a hanging scroll and the name of Kami written on it.

There are several cautionary instructions for installing a household shrine. For example, one should avoid the northeast and southwest corner of the house as seen from the center of the house. When considering the installation of a household shrine, it is important to consult with a reliable *kannushi*.

A charm (*ofuda*) that people obtain from a shrine is solely a symbol and is not *kamizane* in a strict sense. But it can be effective as a target at which everyday prayers are directed. Yamakage Shinto offers people the facility to practice for one hundred days. Then it is recommended to face toward the *ofuda* if there is no *kamidana*, or home altar. It is worth noting that the program of one hundred days training[12] includes prayers, mental concentration, meditation, and sound exercises. As long as people worship with reverence and pray with focused attention, they can open the path to the spirit of Kami.

However, it is ill-advised to collect a variety of charms and worship them. The spirit of Kami that people offer prayers toward has to be determined according to one's own spiritual relationship or spiritual line, of which more will be said in Chapter 8. It is wrong to assume that people can attain more spiritual favor, or grace, if they put several charm cards of well-known Kami at their *kamidana* and offer prayers to all of them. On the contrary, bad influences can result from such an action. We should avoid indiscriminately cramming charm cards from many different shrines into the little shrine at home. When we place charm cards in our home shrine, we should place at the center the card from the shrine that we consider the most noble and which has the closest personal and familial associations.

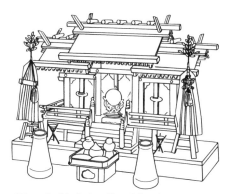

Household shrine (*kamidana*)

Household shrine (*kamidoko*)

CHAPTER 4

The Idea of *Misogi*

(Purification)

Four types of purification (*seimei seichoku*)

The underlying philosophy, indeed the very source of Shinto, is a form of purification that has four aspects. These are best summarized in English by the familiar terms clean, bright, right, and straight. The term "bright" also has the connotation of "happy," while "straight" conveys the idea of "honest." The words seem simple, but together they form the most important first principles for human life, out of which all else that is of value emerges. Clean is expressed in Japanese with the Chinese pronunciation *sei*, bright as *mei*, right as *sei*, and straight as *choku*.

Sometimes the first two concepts are fused together as "clean and bright" (*seimei*) and the second pair as "right and straight" (*seichoku*). Depending upon whom you ask it can be explained differently, but the following is my interpretation:

> **Seimei** means a clean and happy attitude of inner mind, that is, without impurity together with a bright, happy, or clear mind.
>
> **Seichoku** means right action or behavior as well as the social aspect of being right, (that is, not committing any

sin, crime, or offense) and behaving with honesty, openness, and frankness toward others.

To keep in oneself the quality of *seimei* (clean and bright) one has to purify one's mind. There are four ways of doing this:

1. Purification with water.
2. Purification of the body with *haraimono*—the material used for rituals associated with cleansing.
3. The breaking of contact with unclean spirits.
4. Keeping one's thoughts clean.

The first method of purification with water is the original meaning of *misogi*.

Misogi is the cornerstone of Shinto

Misogi is expressed outwardly through the action of bathing in water. The character used to describe *misogi* also implies the physical act of bathing. We can find this character for *misogi* in a caption of the *reigishi* section of an ancient Chinese book, *Gokansho*, where it is written:

> "On March 3rd, at the upper stream on the east side of the river, I cleaned myself. We call it the 'bathing and prayer festival for shen (Chinese for Kami).' "

From this we can tell that the ancient Chinese worshipped their gods or Kami after having bathed themselves.

In Shinto, the authoritative text for *misogi* is found in the story of *misogi harae* practiced by *Izanagi no mikoto*. This story is found in the book, *Kojiki* (The Ancient Chronicles of Japan). In this story it is said that *Izanagi no mikoto* grieved so much for the passing of his wife *Izanami no mikoto*, that he visited Hades, the land of the dead (*yomi no kuni*), only to end up finding her figure totally changed. She was covered with maggots, and he cried out in disgust at her ugliness. When she realized that he had seen her in this horribly transformed state, *Izanami* felt so angry that she chased after him. When *Izanagi* finally managed to escape from her, he practiced *misogi* at Odo of Tachibana at Himuka in Tsukushi—an ancient place of unknown location—at the cross-section of the ocean and river in order to cleanse himself from the impurity of Hades. At that time many Kami were born. It is said that the last three born were *Amaterasu omikami* (sun), *Tsukuyomi no mikoto* (moon), and *Susanoo no mikoto* (wind). This story carries many profound philosophical implications, which I will discuss later.

Misogi was the ritual at the heart of the Shinto ceremony. In the oldest collection of Japanese short poems called *Hyakunin'isshu*, there is a song to mark the purification of summer, which takes place in June in the lunar calendar:

> "The wind is gently blowing through the oak tree beside a brook at twilight. Yes, it is *misogi* season that is the sign of summer."

Summer is the primary season for *misogi* in early Shinto. It was also invariably carried out at the mid-autumn harvest festival, however, and during the prayer festival for the year at mid-winter, known as the winter solstice in the West. It always took place when *Saigu* (or *Itsuki no miya*) is opened at the Ise Shrine, or when *Saiin* (the building for purification) is opened at the Kamo Shrine. *Saigu* is the pure shrine at Ise for the emperor's unmarried virginal daughter who serves *Amaterasu omikami*.

The book *Azuma Kagami* relates that in Kyoto during the Heian period there were seven purification rituals practiced at the seven dry riverbeds. The book also explains that during the Kamakura period a *daimyo* (samurai lord) and his wife practiced *misogi* at the Yui beach. There used to be a prayer ritual for purification read by a *kannushi* or yin/yang master beside the water. This involved brushing people's bodies with special paper objects, named *hitogata*, or paper cut in a human shape (see Chapter 5). Often, the participants bathed themselves or poured water over the body in order to expel the uncleanness (*kegare*).

This type of purification of the body was also practiced twice by the present emperor. At the time of *daijosai*, the imperial enthronement ceremony, he bathed himself in water for purification purposes.

Misogi was originally practiced in the ocean

Since the Japanese are an ocean tribe who came to their island nation from across the seas, I believe that the original *misogi* was probably practiced at the ocean. In the great purification words, *oharai no kotoba*, or in its abridged form, the purification words, *misogi harai no kotoba*, several ocean Kami assume the role of Kami who exorcise transgressions, offences, and uncleanness. *Misogi* in the ocean still forms part of a modern program of Shinto-based exercises. It is also practiced in some localities where ancient customs have been preserved. In such places the spiritual leader who performs these rituals enters the ocean himself to practice *misogi*.

Another type of *misogi* is found at the Amano Shrine in Kishu, where people carry a portable shrine (*mikoshi*) to the ocean beach and pour sea water over it for ritual cleansing. A further type of *misogi* is found at the festival of the Manazuru Shrine in Kanagawa where a portable shrine floats on the surface of the sea. There are many festivals of this type throughout Japan. We can also witness people soaking their feet in the sea in an event known as *hamauri*, which means "going down to the beach." This is done on March 3rd in Okinawa, and through this timeless ritual we catch glimpses of the ancient culture of these islands.

Some people still now assert that sea water has greater purifying power, and we still have the custom of putting salt beside the place where we wash off water deposits with fresh water. We also purify with salt. All these customs are probably remnants of people's strong nostalgia and desire for sea water.

Additionally, the best place for cleansing seems to be the spot where the river flows into the sea, and this suggests a connection between *misogi* and the ocean.

Several Kami were born through the *misogi* practiced by *Izanagi no mikoto*. Among them are: *Sokotsuwatatsumi no kami*; *Nakatsuwatatsumi no kami*; *Uwatsuwatatsumi no kami*; *Sokotsutsuo no mikoto*; *Nakatsutsuo no mikoto*; and *Uwatsutsuo no mikoto*.

It is worth noting here that the name *Watatsumi* relates to the ocean. *Soko*, *naka*, and *uwa* mean respectively "bottom, middle, and top." The presence of such names suggests a continuing awareness of the ocean's existence at different levels, or hidden depths. Note also that *mikoto* is another way to give a name for Kami.

These six Kami are enshrined in the Sumiyoshi Shrine, a type that can be found at Osaka, Fukuoka, and various other locations. These historic shrines are located at the mouth of the river into the ocean.

River water is fresh and symbolizes the masculine. Ocean water symbolizes the feminine. The mouth where these two meet is the symbol of intercourse between man and woman. The two Kami *Izanagi* and *Izanami* shared the intercourse of *Mito* (*Mito no maguwai*), which resulted in the birth of many Kami offspring. *Mito* is a combination of two words—*mi(zu)* and *to*; *mi(zu)* meaning "water" and *to* meaning "door." This symbolically suggests the merging of two waters—indeed, the intercourse of two waters. Since many Kami were born after the *misogi* practiced by *Izanagi no mikoto*, I am inclined to say that this *misogi* suggests the intercourse between man and woman, implying rebirth. This is why I believe that the mouth of the river where fresh water meets the sea is the appropriate place for *misogi* to be practiced.

This does not mean that *misogi* practiced at other places is inherently less valuable. Whether *misogi* is practiced at a river or at a waterfall or in the bathroom, it is still *misogi*. However, *misogi* at the ocean, and particularly at the mouth of a river where it meets the ocean, is the one I particularly value as the most appropriate and original form.

Misogi practice at the ocean near *Kireigu*

The conceptual level of *misogi*

Misogi is not simply a matter of washing and cleansing the body. When the physical body is made clean by water, our heart and mind are purified at the same time. The act of washing our hands before worshiping at a shrine is about more than the magical cleansing power of water. We also make a distinction within ourselves between the secular and the sacred by that act, and thus we change our attitude and our mindset. In so doing, we wash away uncleanness. We purify our heart and mind so that we may connect with the spirit of Kami with a heart and mind that is clean, bright, right, and straight. This is the most important goal of *misogi*.

The *misogi* story of *Izanagi no mikoto* in the *Kojiki* not only tells of cleaning the body but also contains other significant hidden meanings. It tells us that when *Izanagi no mikoto* arrived at *Odono Awagihara*, the place for *misogi*, he threw away various things he carried and wore at the time. Each time he threw something away a new Kami was born. Let us try to discover the meaning of this story. This account contains several significant details:

1) When *Izanagi* nailed his walking stick to the ground, *Tsukitatsufunado no kami* was born. This symbolizes the completion of the long journey of illusion. His walking stick symbolizes the journey of life until the finishing point. By nailing it into the ground, he marks the journey's conclusion. A port, or *funado*, is also a symbol of this journey.

2) When he removed his sash, *Michinonagachiha no kami* was born. The removal of the sash symbolizes the sense of contented awareness at the end of the journey. *Michi* is the word for road and *naga* the word for long. Together they signify the process of looking back over life's long road.

3) When he removed his *mo* (a cover over traditional Japanese long pants), *Tokiokashi no kami* (Kami who puts down Time) was born. The removal of *mo* symbolizes the lifting of the world of illusion he had been living in, and *mo* itself represents the relativity of time.

4) When he removed the cloth from his upper body, *Wazurainoushi no kami* was born—the term means the "center of worries." The naked upper body represents release from worries.

5) When he took off his *fundoshi* (traditional Japanese loincloth), *Michimata no kami* (Kami of the Forked Road) was born. This means that *Izanagi* was freed from doubt and vacillation when encountering life's forked roads. The area of the groin revealed by the removal of his *fundoshi* corresponds to the forked road, and is purified through the ritual of *misogi*.

6) When he took off the crown, *Akiguinoushi no kami* (Kami who is Tired of Biting) was born. By throwing the crown, he is declaring that he is tired of biting into the power, status, and privileges he had previously enjoyed. The shape of an open mouth for eating—or biting—is seen to resemble the shape of an inverted crown.

7) When he threw away his *tamaki* (the armbands holding up his sleeves), *Okizakaru no kami* and *Hezakaru no kami* (Kami who becomes more Deeply Detached and Kami who Steps Aside) were born. This means that *Izanagi* disowned those around him who clung to his arms; that is, his vassals or "hangers on." He graduated from illusion, and put into perspective his relationships with people and his surroundings. This is precisely the idea of *misogi*.

After this, *Izanagi no mikoto* rinsed his body with water, and more Kami were born:

8) After rinsing, *Yasomagatsuhi no kami* (Kami who Causes many Disasters) and *Omagatsuhi no kami* (Kami causing Great Disasters) were born. These are unclean Kami, and their emergence symbolizes the expulsion of dirt from the body through washing.

9) In order to heal and repair disasters, *Kannaobi no kami* (Kami for Divine Correction), *Onaobi no kami* (Kami for Great Correction), and *Izume no kami* (the Solemn Female Kami) subsequently appeared.

10) When he cleansed his lower body, at the bottom, middle, and surface of the water, the following Kami appeared:

Sokotsuwatatsumi no kami (Kami at the Bottom of the Ocean)
Sokotsutsuno no mikoto (Prince at the Bottom)
Nakatsuwatatsumi no kami (Kami at the Middle of the Ocean)
Nakatsutsuno no mikoto (Prince at the Middle)
Uwatsuwatatsumi no kami (Kami at the Surface of the Ocean)
Uwatsutsuno no mikoto (Prince at the Surface of the Ocean).

These Kami are spirit of Kami with the power of cleansing *kegare* (uncleanness). In other words, they are incarnations of the great purifying power of the universe. These names are slightly different from the ones used in both the *misogi* purification words (*misogi harai no kotoba*) and the great purification words (*oharai no kotoba*). There, the Kami are called *Haraedo no okami* (Great Kami at the Purification Place).

In this way through *misogi*, *Izanagi no mikoto* returned to his true self, completely refreshed, his nakedness symbolizing release. Afterwards, he underwent a spiritual cleansing, and through the mystery of *musubi* (meaning "generative") he bore three noble children. Here, the characters literally mean "three pillars (columns) of noble children." The Japanese word for pillar is sometimes used as a synonym for Kami. The three pillars are *Amaterasu omikami* (sun), *Tsukuyomi no mikoto* (moon), and *Susanoo no mikoto* (wind).

There are profound symbolic meanings hidden here, too. *Susanoo no mikoto* represents the physical act of creation, meaning "a healthy body of flesh which can act with courage and composure." *Tsukuyomi no mikoto* represents mental and psychological creativity, meaning "gaining profound mental sensitivity and heart with a mind of peace, reverence, and serenity." *Amaterasu omikami* represents spiritual creativity, and means "realization of justice and fairness of heart and opening oneself to becoming spiritually clean, bright, right, and honest."

Through this myth, therefore, the idea of *misogi* is symbolically explored in depth. *Misogi* has spiritual and mystical meanings far beyond the simple meaning of bathing in the water. Purification with water can be found in many different world religions, such as Christianity, Hinduism, and others. In Shinto, *misogi* has to do with the root of the idea of being clean, bright, right, and straight—it therefore has an extremely important spiritual meaning.

Purifying materials

There is another means of purifying the body in the Shinto tradition, which involves the use of purifying materials. We are told that in the ancient style of *misogi harai* (purification and cleansing), participants rolled up their sleeves with a cotton sash and held some plants called *torimono* (meaning "things to hold") to perform *misogi*. These plants were sedge plants, a hemp leaf, a miscanthus plant, or summer greens. It is probable that the body was stroked with *torimono* to let the plant absorb all kinds of sin, faults, uncleanness, or *mononoke*, meaning vengeful ghosts, specters, and low-energy vibrations. The plants were then thrown into the river.

In the *Kujikongen*, the book that describes and explains imperial court events, we can find the following short poem:

> *Wishing for all my thoughts to perish,*
> *I cleansed myself by stroking myself*
> *with hemp leaf again and again and again.*

Thus people have practiced cleansing with *haraimono* (materials for cleansing) made of natural products since ancient times. In the past, if people could not find a bathroom when they went to a shrine for worship, they plucked out green leaves from trees (any kinds were fine) to wipe their hands, then threw the leaves away.

These *haraimono* have strong effects, particularly when removing *kegare* (impurities) or *mononoke*. The term *mononoke* is usually used in combination with the practice of the so-called masters of yin and yang. Apparently it also has been used in earlier times, even as far back as the Nara period (710–94). During the Heian period (794–1185), the word meant "spirit of death," or a vengeful spirit. But generally it means invisible beings made of subtle matter. These spirits can be both good and bad, but they are usually of low level or mischievous character, akin to the negative products of malicious thoughts. People with a strongly psychic ability can see *mononoke* as a miasmic or fog-like presence, or experience feelings of cold or nausea.

Kegare is the negative energy emitted from dead, decaying bodies, or negative vibrations emitted by wicked minds or evil spirits. This energy can be harnessed to induce sickness or even death in others. (The attitude of considering menstrual blood, feces, or urine as *kegare* comes from Buddhism. It is not originally a Shinto idea.)

In order to purify these semi-material energies, physical materials such as *hitogata* paper or *harai nusa* (purifying wand) are used. We purify people or things by absorbing their negative energy.

One can find a thick rope (*shimenawa*—the plaited straw rope to protect the sacred space) across the front of a shrine building above the heads of the devotees. This is for attracting and attaching bad vibrations, *kegare*, and any other negative elements to the rope in order to protect the shrine. Therefore, when changing *shimenawa*, one experiences powerful unclean influences, such as malicious and poisonous thoughts, on contact with the discarded rope. The rope should be changed at any festival or special Shinto ceremony, especially on occasions when the shrine is being purified. It should also be changed at least one other time each year.

We also experience strong *kegare* at funeral services. In these situations, we use the *harai nusa* only once, throwing it away after each usage, so we therefore need many *harai nusa*. The way a funeral is conducted in Yamakage Shinto is to begin with the purification of the dead body. Then, the *chinkon* service involves settling the *nigimi-tama*[13] (one of the four different soul levels of a human being) down onto an unvarnished wooden object known as a *mitamashiro*. This literally means "the temporary container of the spirit." The spirit of dead people is considered to be present within this wooden object, therefore after the person's death it serves as the spiritual antenna for the spirit to come down when a ceremony is held.

After the *chinkon* service, there is a vigil service at night. This is followed by the service for bidding farewell to the dead and a house purification service. Afterwards, the purification of the fireplace for cremation occurs and then finally the service for welcoming home the ashes. So, altogether, seven to ten *harai nusa* will be used and thrown away.

Some *kannushi* claim that *harai nusa* itself never becomes unclean because it is *yorishiro* for *Haraedo no okami*. In other words, it acts as the spiritual antenna upon which *Haraedo no okami* descends in order to manifest its presence. But *harai nusa* is a physical material for attracting *kegare* (uncleanness), and so I believe the same one should not be repeatedly used, especially when we deal with a very strong *kegare*. We therefore have to observe the rule of using it once only. With this principle in mind, *harai nusa* at the front of the shrine is changed to a new one every month or at each important ritual service.

Cutting off contact with unclean spirits

As I will say again later, it is important to be aware that the spirit world contains unclean or evil spirits as well as pure spirits of high status. If we get influenced by unclean spirits, we cannot keep ourselves clean and bright—no matter how much we clean our physical body.

One form of unclean spirit is the ancestral spirit (*innenrei*) that follows people because of their familial connection. Other spirits (*ban-rei*), however, are those which individuals happen to attract to themselves. When affected by spirits that do not relate to kinship—for example, the spirits that take possession of casual passers-by—it is only necessary to engage in purification to be rid of them. This type of spirit sometimes pretends to be a friend of the possessed person. In the case of the spirits related to familial connections, we must find the reason for the possession, no matter how apparently trivial it might be, and then provide solutions for the spirit's demands.

To achieve the clarity of perception necessary in such circumstances, the services of a reliable *kannushi* or spiritual teacher should be sought. The possessing spirit must be convinced to depart by a process of right thinking. Also, a memorial service may be held for that spirit, which includes a purifying ritual. It is crucial that the person who conducts the ritual is motivated by right thinking, has integrity, and possesses the ability to communicate with spirits. If he is not competent in all of these areas, then the danger of adverse effects can be increased. Above all, it is important always to attempt to lead a clean and bright life, so we can prevent unnecessarily inviting the influence of malevolent spirits. It is particularly important that we have the right spiritual knowledge. If we indulge ourselves in evil passions and lead a wicked life, we also will naturally attract low vibrating spirits that are in accord with our own low vibration.

Keeping our thinking "clean and bright"

As I mentioned above, it is important to purify our thoughts in order not to be affected by low vibrating spirits. To do that, we must put our chaotic thoughts in order and learn the truth. This is the ultimate goal of *misogi*.

Purifying the mind means purifying our words and thoughts, and straightening our way of thinking and the way we experience reality. Therefore, it is necessary to read spiritual books that inspire and to listen to teachers or masters who have undergone disciplined, spiritual training.

It is not good enough, however, merely to understand books and lectures with the rational part of the brain. Of equal, indeed if not greater, importance are purity of mind and heart. An aesthetic sensibility that is receptive to cleanness and brightness is also essential. In order to achieve this, it is important to take time to examine one's own heart and mind, one's feelings and motives. For it is always so easy for human minds to expand lazily and limitlessly, and in so doing to lose stability. We must therefore keep our mind firmly at the center of our body (*tanden* or *tantien*) that is the center of our true self, to avoid its falling into a state of imbalance. We shall explore this further below in the context of the exercises designed to preserve a state of equilibrium and well-being in the three levels of consciousness represented by body, mind, and spirit. The concept of *harai* is linked intimately to the idea of *misogi* and is therefore the subject of the next chapter.

CHAPTER 5

The Idea of *Harai*

What is *harai*?

It is said that Shinto begins and ends with *harai*. This statement does not simply apply to practice and ceremony. *Harai* as an idea is the very center of Shinto philosophy.

There are many interpretations of the term *harai*. One original interpretation means repaying reciprocal obligations and so restoring balance. This interpretation is taken from two Japanese words, *hareau* = *hare* (晴) + *au* (合), or *harashiau* = *harashi* + *au*. Both mean "clearing away each other."

Both of these are compound words, and according to the degree of the misdemeanor or offence, people give offerings to Kami in order to clear away their transgressions. The same pronunciation of the word *harai*, one that uses a different character, used to have the meaning of shaking dust off in order to become clean or to make things clean. This concept is an almost perfect match for the idea of clearing away transgression through atonement by purification. And so, as the two concepts merged, the two characters—"shaking off dust" and "cleansing through atonement" were confused and became interchangeable.

Another interpretation of *harai* is *haruhi* (the character *haru* 張 means "expand, fill;" *hi* 霊 means "spirit"). The season *haru*, meaning "spring" in Japanese, implies expansion, the expansion of vitality or life energy. That is, it gives vitality and force to spirit and soul (*reikon*).

We may therefore safely conclude that the word *harai* contains within itself the deeper meanings that form the basis of Shinto. The first of these is that we become spiritually clean by washing away our errors and misdeeds. Secondly, we achieve this goal of cleanness by making offerings for expiation for our past actions. Then, through this work, we renew the vitality of our own body and mind—this is the third meaning of *harai*. I will talk later about the reason why we treat these mistakes/offences/*kegare* (uncleanness) like material things.

Harai with heaven or celestial cleansing

We are told that in *harai* there have been three categories of heaven, earth, and humanity since ancient times. The expression, heaven, earth, and humanity is certainly influenced by Chinese ideas. Nonetheless, it is a useful place to begin an explanation of *harai* in Shinto.

The purification with *harai* through heaven involves receiving spiritual light from the spirit of Kami, the spirit of the word (*kotodama*) or the spirit of sound (*otodama*).

The *harai* of spiritual light from the spirit of Kami signifies the worship of Kami and cleansing of oneself by receiving sacred vibrations. To adapt this process to the needs of the general public, we employ *harai* with *harai nusa* (see the illustration in Chapter 3). The power of *harai* with heaven comes from the sacred cleansing power of *Haraedo no okami*, who was born of *Izanagi no mikoto* through the practice of *misogi*. People call for that power in order to be cleansed—as was described in detail in the previous chapter.

Most people are under the impression that they have finished all purification work after doing *harai* with *harai nusa*, but this is not the case. This is only a preliminary *harai* ritual for making contact with Kami. The work for real purification, in the true sense of the word, comes after the necessary amount of cleanness is achieved with *harai nusa*. At this point, one offers prayers to Kami once again in order to be cleansed in a true sense. This is known as the original way of purification through the spiritual light of Kami spirit.

The concept of the spirit of the word is a very important idea in Japanese Shinto. I shall not go into details about this now, but I shall only mention here that the spirit of the word is the word that has mystical power, impregnated with the grace (that is to say the authority, glory, and virtue) of the spirit of Kami. The ancient Japanese considered the power of the spirit of the word as very important. In volume 13 of *Man'yoshu*, a collection of short songs from early Japan, Kakinomoto Hitomaro, a famous poet, sang:

> *The country of Shikishima Yamato is truly blessed,*
> *because the spirit of the word helps it.*

In volume 5, Yamanoue Okura sang:

> *It has been said since mythological times that the country*
> *of Yamato is the beloved land of Emperor Kami*
> *where the spirit of the word is flourishing.*

Thus, it has been felt that Japan enjoys the protection and blessing of the spirit of the word. Japanese short poems have reflected the music of that spirit, for the Japanese of old believed that they could make people happy by saying good words. The words which make people happy are called *kotohogi*, meaning "celebration words."

The spirit of the word is not only the word that comes from the spirit of Kami, but also the word for awakening that spirit. In Shinto, the great purifying words (*oharai no kotoba*; see Appendix 1) are the best way of representing this concept. These Shinto ritual words can be found in the book *Engishiki*, and are also known as the purifying words of Nakatomi (*Nakatomi no harae*). This has generally been handed down throughout the ages as a chant used in facing Kami. In the Edo period (1600–1867), a master of Ise presented this chant to the Japanese public and advocated its widespread use. People repeated this prayer one hundred or even one thousand times, hence it is also known as the "one hundred purifications" or the "one thousand purifications." Kurozumi Munetada (1780–1850), a religious man who lived around the end of the Edo period, continued this practice and established it as the systematic training method of the Kurozumi Sect. I should say here that the spiritual power concealed in the great purifying words (*oharai no kotoba*) is widely acknowledged to be immense.

The mystery of the great purifying words (*oharai no kotoba*)

At the age of eighteen, I began chanting the great purifying words from memory. This was 1943, in the Showa era (1926–89) when the people of Japan were living through a period that has been described as one of difficulties without precedent since ancient times. Japan was enduring large-scale air raid attacks in Tokyo and many other cities.

During that year, I was near death and bedridden with pulmonary tuberculosis. I actually experienced a temporary death. Fortunately, I was revived with a miracle, which I will explain later. I began chanting the great purifying words while I was confined to bed because a wise old man, Shinjiro Baba, had recommended them to me.

This chanting is not short, and many of the chanted words deceptively resemble each other, and so for a person like me who has a poor memory it was not easy to learn by heart. I needed to look at the printed text of those words again and again. It took many months for me to memorize the words in their entirety.

When I had finally been able to commit the words to memory and recite them in full, a miracle occurred. I recovered my health to the point that I was able to pray in a sitting posture. I sat up in bed in the formal position used to chant the great purification words. Needless to say, it was hard work for a patient at death's door, and it took seven minutes to complete the entire prayer. In the beginning, my condition was so severe that I could not bear reading out the words even once in full. But when I had fully memorized them, I suddenly found the strength to recite. And after several months of practice, I began to gather strength and energy in my abdomen, so I was able to chant the entire words three times with a rich and resonant voice that seemed to emerge from the center of my belly.

In those days neither antibiotics, nor good and nourishing food, nor vitamins needed for a sick body were available. Despite these hardships, my health improved, seemingly because of the great purification words. I cannot think of any other reason for this miraculous improvement.

Soon, I was able to walk in a standing position, so I dedicated myself to practicing walking. Whilst walking, I chanted the great purification words in order to gain a state of mind free from all distracting ideas and thoughts. At the beginning, I decided to walk the distance equivalent to the chanting time of one entire set of prayer words, but I gradually increased the distance to two chanting times of the entire prayer, and then three times. Eventually I was able to walk the distance of ten entire chants.

Since we chant these words with energy from the abdomen, it naturally creates the repetition of deep breathing from the belly: this way of breathing is called the "long breathing method" (*okinagaho*) in Shinto. Through this breathing, the power in the physical body is increased. Furthermore, if one chants this prayer with the whole heart, it is possible to erase all unnecessary worldly thoughts and eventually reach a state of mind that is void of *all* ideas and thoughts. Then all uncleanness and impurity within the brain disappears. I have to say, however, the power of *kotodama* is more than simply that of physical matter. This mysterious power cleanses the bad vibrations of malice and poison (*magatsuhi*) in the body. It is a source of spiritual energy, and sometimes even the inspiration that unleashes the power of spiritual healing.

The great incantation (*daijinju*) of Yamakage Shinto

In Yamakage Shinto, there is an even more mysterious and powerful spiritual incantation passed down from ancient times. It is the incantation *ajimarikan*, or in its original and more authentic form, *ajimarikamu*: the syllable *mu* is pronounced as an *n* with the mouth tightly shut.

This incantation is of ancient provenance, and the meaning is not clear. There are many different interpretations, but all of these to my mind lack precision or conviction. In Yamakage Shinto, we teach this incantation as the spirit of the word, which has existed since the beginning of heaven and earth—this means the point of origin of the universe.

We hear countless stories about people who have had various

spiritual experiences through chanting this incantation. When we hold a memorial service in honor of each soul of a dead person or pray for activation of *jirei* (self spirit; in other words, the higher self), we chant this incantation. Our tradition tells us that you can acquire supernatural power if you chant it a million times.

Harai of the spirit of sounds (*otodama*)

Harai of the spirit of sounds means purification through the use of music.

People often report that they sense a room to be very pure and clean after good music has been performed there. In Japan, I believe that the courtly music known as *kagura* from ancient times has quite a high level of purifying vibration, somewhat akin to the European tradition of organ music.

In Shinto, the drum is used at prayer and represents the sound of a big ocean wave breaking back and forth on the beach. It is said that the rhythm or vibration of the drum has the power of purification. The purpose of music at Shinto ceremonies is therefore far from merely decorative.

We do not need scientific proof of the beneficial effects of music, because we experience them for ourselves. We have experienced that when good music is played, the fermentation of *sake* (Japanese rice wine) improves in flavor and taste. There are also reports that plants respond positively to music, which can be used to aid their growth. It is my own belief, based on personal experience and the insights of others, that musical vibration contains a mysterious power.

Harai with earth and salt

In the process of cleansing with earth, we note that there are three elements involved: water, soil, and salt. Cleansing through water is of course *misogi*, which we explored in the previous chapter.

We can say that purification with earth is practiced when we use sand from a beach, or soil taken from the shrine's compound or a similar sacred place in order to purify the premises. We sometimes spread these purifying agents all over the premises. Another example of this form of purification can be seen at the Omiwa Shrine in Nara, where an offering of the soil from Mt. Shintai is made for the ceremony of purifying a building site (*jichinsai*).

Salt is important as a cleansing and purifying agent. We can witness examples of using salt as a purifying agent in several areas of life. One such example is when salt is sprinkled over the person coming home from a funeral, or when it is scattered over the sumo-wrestling arena, or when it is piled up at the entrance of a sushi shop. The reason for these customs in Japan cannot simply be attributed to a Japanese love of salt or to the fact that we are an ocean people, although these are both relevant. There are other, more subtle reasons.

Salt is the major component of ocean water. Ocean water is the very basis and essence of life. The components of human body fluid—

sodium (natrium), magnesium, potassium (kalium) and calcium—found in ocean water are essential elements for the proper functioning of the human body, and naturally harvested sea salt contains these in good and proper balance.

Salt is also the king of the cooking spices. Moreover, it prevents food from decaying. All this said, it is clear that salt is very significant, giving vitality to the inside and outside of the human body. It is the gift from the great nature.

Furthermore, salt is the element that has mystical purifying powers beyond the physical effects just described. People who use salt for purification can feel its power. Since ancient times, the Japanese have revered the power of salt, and they have used it for purifying houses or land—and on many other occasions where purification is necessary.

Harai with human beings

There are two methods for the cleansing of the human spirit. The first of these is known as "Cleansing with a purifying object shaped to resemble a human being" (*katashiro no harai*). The second is "Cleansing through purifying fire" (*imibi no harai*). *Imi* means "sacred" in this sense, so *imibi* is the sacred and special fire used in order to purify uncleanness.

In *katashiro*, materials typically used for rendering the human form are steel, plants, tree bark, and clay (*hani*). The most popular material is paper, referred to as *hitogata*.

Types of *katashiro*: bark and paper (*kami-hitogata*)

Paper was invented in China and introduced to Japan during the Nara period (710–94). It was a very precious material and was presented to the shrine as an offering. In the beginning, a quire of paper was placed between the ends of bamboo poles and the tops were tied with linen cloth. Later on, paper hangings (*shide*) were attached in ways that created the shape of *gohei*. Later on, this *gohei* was used as *yorishiro* or *himorogi*, the spiritual antenna by which the spirit of Kami can descend and manifest its presence (see Chapter 3). Eventually, the *gohei* itself became the symbol of Kami. In Shinto we assume that "Kami and human beings are of the same shape," so it is quite logical that the shape of *gohei* took on the human shape.

As the production of *gohei* increased, paper gradually supplanted the more ancient uses of bark from the Japanese cypress or cedar and plants such as hemp and straw.

An original way of referring to *katashiro* was to use the word

the paper after having rubbed the affected part of the sick person with it, we find turbid black ash left over after the burning. Sometimes even, when we are preparing the *hitogata*, it can become tainted before it is used, because it has already attracted and absorbed the bad vibration of the afflicted person for whom it has been made. *Katashiro harai*, the purification with *hitogata*, has a mysterious dimension, which is hard to understand for a rational mind. *Hitogata* are also used in the four corners of a room to protect the space against bad vibrations. It absorbs bad vibrations produced in a room where people are quarreling or expressing prejudice and selfish thoughts. When these *hitogata* are burnt, the flame might turn into a poisonous green and the ashes a turbid black.

Fire is also seen to have a strong purifying power, for it was considered to be Kami, not only in Japan but also for many other ancient people. Throughout history, Kami of fire has been treated as the chief or primary Kami. Fire was viewed as the source of life for ancient people, because they knew that it kept the body warm, just as the absence of it in the dead body made the body cold. For the ancients, "fire" (*hi* in Japanese) was "spirit" (this is also *hi* in Japanese) as well as "sun" (also pronounced as *hi*), which brought them warm rays. Moreover, fire has a wonderful power— it lights up the darkness, cooks food, and creates pottery and metals.

One drawback of fire is, of course, that it burns everything up, but the fire that burns the crop field has the compensating power to create new crop production. The Japanese named the Fire-Kami burning in the crop field as *Honokagutsuchi no kami* (both *ho* and *kagu* mean "fire," and *tsuchi* means "soil," "earth," or "land"), and the field fire at night as *Honoyagihayao no kami* (*ya* means "night," *hayao* means "fast man").

Ancient people sensed the mysterious nature and vitality of fire. They thought that in fire there was an unclean fire (*magatsubi*) as well as a purifying fire power (*imibi*). *Imibi* cleans the body, and we pray to Kami each time we start an *imibi* fire.

Since ancient times, it has been thought that fire is the most powerful purifying agent, particularly for spiritual purification. It follows from this that we should burn the bad vibrations absorbed during the *katashiro* cleansing practice. Therefore, we cannot really separate *katashiro* cleansing from *imibi* cleansing. The two processes go together.

In Yamakage Shinto, we practice the fire ceremony in order to purify the souls of our ancestors or relatives that are still unclean. We call this ritual *joensai*, the ritual service of purifying fire.

Up to this point I have discussed the practice of *harai* on its three levels of heaven, earth, and humanity. Among all these purification practices the purification with the sound of words, salt, and fire—have been considered as the "three great hidden methods for purifying spirits" from ancient times.

What is *kegare*?

I have thus far discussed *harai* in detail and explained it as the basis of Shinto. Now I have to stress that underlying the theory of *harai* is Shinto's unique approach to humanity.

In both the great purification words (*oharai no kotoba*) and the *misogi* purification words (*misogi harai no kotoba*), which is the abridged version of the great purification words, human error and uncleanness are considered coterminous. It is believed that we can completely remove error and uncleanness by washing them away with *misogi* or purifying them with *harai*. They are treated, therefore, as if they were forms of material "dirt" that can be expunged by washing.

It is believed that as long as we completely remove sin, fault, and uncleanness by washing them away through *misogi* or *harai* then that will be enough. Certain types of uncleanness are widely viewed in human cultures as having a material extension: they are not mere products of the mind because they have an impact, physical as well as mental, on their surroundings. This is why we treat them as if they were material substance and deal with them accordingly.

It would be a complex and scholarly task to analyze the nature of "sin" as it is found in classical Japanese writing, if indeed the word "sin" is even applicable. I shall abstain from that task for now and merely present the essence of the Shinto approach. In short, it is this: **Shinto does not preach the idea of absolute sin**. Unlike the teaching of original sin found in other religions, Shinto expresses the concept of **no sin**, or to put it more positively, the inherent goodness of nature. In Shinto, the essence of spirit-soul within human beings is a gift from Kami, so it is considered flawless and perfect even if humans err. The error is contained in the action itself, and it will not follow the person around forever if purification is obtained. In Shinto, it is said that once we wash away error in a river or ocean through the purification of *misogi*, it will vanish completely with the dirt of the body that is washed away. In the great purification words, there is a line as reference to the "various kinds of sins which we commit by mistake." Therefore, in the theory of Shinto, error and fault are mistakes committed by immature souls, not "sins" in the Western sense of the word.

Shinto treats these faults as if they were forms of matter. From the spiritual standpoint, errors committed consciously or faults that are unconscious are both actions that become a form of semi-substance. This exists as invisible memory or as a record either in the innermost level of consciousness or within the physical body. They can be also recorded in space, in the earth, and in the universal memory, or collective unconscious. When a spiritually sensitive person stands in an old battlefield, he or she can sense the carnage there as if it were still real. The same thing could happen in the case of errors and faults. Therefore, it follows that we can wash away error, fault, and uncleanness through the use of spiritual energy or vibrations. These methods of purification are part of the original tradition of *koshinto*.

It is important to remember that in Shinto the nature of human beings is considered to be essentially good. Shinto does not preach that human beings are burdened with original sin and can only be saved through faith. Even if we commit a sin, as long as we remove or dissolve the sin through purification, we will be restored to cleanness, which is the balance of body, mind, and soul. For purification is the cornerstone of Shinto.

Human beings have the potential to become Kami

As we explore the *koshinto* tradition to its deepest level, we discover that human beings have the potential to become Kami.

To be sure, in our present form we, as human beings, are most definitely not Kami, but within us there is *naohinomitama*. This means "original, pure, and upright spirit," "the spark of divine light," or "the offspring of Kami" emerging out of the creator Kami of the universe (see Chapter 6). This spirit has the same quality as Kami, but on an infinitesimally smaller scale. This is *wakemitama* or *bunrei*—the spirit-child of Kami, like the single metaphysical entity of a monad—akin to the bud of a plant. It is the task of humans to nurture that bud so as eventually to "become Kami."

In the sacred texts handed down to Yamakage Shinto, we can find the following expression: "I who have been manifest in this world as one spirit reflect four lights of *daigenrei* (the great original spirit—the creator Kami of the universe)." The spiritual light of Kami dwells in the core of our spirit-soul.

Therefore, even though human beings are tainted with sin, faults, or uncleanness while living in this world, they can rise to the rank of Kami. However, to do so they must reflect on this uncleanness and cleanse themselves, by the so-called "adjustment of sight and hearing."

They must show continuous improvement and progress as they aim at eventually rising to this high rank of Kami. These two spiritual processes are known as *shuri kosei*, or renovation and maintenance, and *seisei kaiku*, which means birth and growth, transformation and development—in other words, the whole process of creation. This is the human way.

Certainly we cannot become Kami simply through natural growth. We need spiritual training and exercises such as *misogi* and *chinkon* (see Chapter 8). We also need to practice the work of love and charity in order to develop a clean and pure character.

The idea of *musubi*

Musubi means to unite or bind together. The meaning of each character used for this word is generate-spirit in the *Nihonshoki* (Chronicles of Japan) and generate-nestle-sun in *Kojiki* (Ancient Chronicles of Japan). We can find another significant use of *musubi* in the names of Kami: *Takamimusubi* and *Kamimusubi*. These appear after *Amenominaka-nushi no kami*, the creator of the universe. So, from this we can tell that the concept of *musubi* must have a deep spiritual meaning.

Musu has another written character, signifying "steam" or "brew," which gives it the meaning of fermentation. Through the process of fermentation, rice or wheat is transformed into something entirely different—*sake*—so *musu* signifies this phenomenon—and by extension other transformatory processes. It also signifies sudden birth, as in the phrase *koke musu* (literally, "moss grow"), which describes the way in which the moss plant emerges suddenly on the surface of a rock.

Hi as *bi* in *musubi* means "fire" (*hi*) and "spirit" (*hi*)—the source of life that I discussed earlier—a phonetic rule in Japanese language creates this sound change from *hi* to *bi*.

We may conclude from all this that the concept of *musubi* signifies the proliferation of life and spirit. *Musubi* (or unification) of man and woman also entails the procreation of life and spirit-soul (*reikon*), and so we call children *musuko* (boy) and *musume* (girl).

In Shinto, the very process of creating and giving birth to life and spirit is described as *musubi* and we place it in very high regard. In other words, the basic religious idea of Shinto is the continuous process of creation. When we apply this principle to an individual spirit-soul, we see that *musubi* is the process of work through which each person generates, grows, transforms, and develops *naohinomitama* (the innermost pure spirit), making his or her spirit grow and become strong. This means that the first task involves the creating of the body, which is attained through diligent care of bodily health. The second task is the creating of heart and mind, or psychological growth. Thirdly, there is the creating of the spirit, that is to say the purification of spirit-soul.

Shinto views as harmful everything that obstructs the work of creation and cultivation (*seisei kaiku*) and creation and development (*seisei hatten*). Everything that helps this work, by contrast, is deemed to be good. Shinto encourages a cheerful way of life, not a distorted one, and it views life as about the pursuit of happiness rather than being constrained by rigorous admonitions or dogmatic rules concerning supposed "sin."

Therefore in Shinto there is no doctrine of absolute and final salvation. Human beings continue to grow. Human beings keep growing throughout their lives, and after their lives on earth they go to the other world (see Chapter 7) and continue living for renovation and maintenance, or *shuri kosei*. Eventually, they may keep growing until they eventually become Kami.

CHAPTER 6

Koshinto

Theory of One Spirit, Four Souls

The philosophy of one spirit, four souls (*ichirei shikon*)

In *koshinto* the philosophy of one spirit, four souls (*ichirei shikon*) has been handed down to the modern age. There are some slight differences in character and interpretation among the different Shinto traditions, but the understandings are generally similar to one another.

One spirit (*ichirei*)

This is also called **naohinomitama** 直日霊 (the three characters in this word mean: straight [*nao*], sun [*hi*], and spirit [*tama*])

Four souls (*shikon*)

THE MANIFESTED SOULS:

> **aramitama** 荒魂 (*ara* means: rough, wild, unruly, gross, and [*mi*]*tama*: soul)
>
> **nigimitama** 和魂 (*nigi* means: harmony, and [*mi*]*tama*: soul)

THE HIDDEN SOULS:

> **sachimitama** 幸魂 (*sachi* means: happy, and [*mi*]*tama*: soul)
>
> **kushimitama** 奇魂 (*kushi* means: mysterious, magical, powerful, and [*mi*]*tama*: soul).

This concept is the underlying philosophy of the universe, the world of plants and animals and each individual living creature, including all human beings.

First I will present here the *ichirei shikon* of the whole universe.

In Yamakage Shinto, the whole universe is called "universe of the great circle" (*daikanu*).

The great spirit of the universe of the great circle
THE FOUR SOULS:

kushimitama The work of the original power stimulating creativity and birth; transforming ideas into actual form.

sachimitama The work of harmonizing the Universe.

nigimitama The work of controlling the activity of the Universe, giving form to generated things and embodying them. The work of making energy permeate all things and give motion to the universe.

aramitama The work of manifesting the individual in the physical world and maintaining the individual organism. The work of destroying everything, causing new life to emerge.

We can interpret that the lineage of all Kami in the myth of *Kojiki* and *Nihonshoki* also follows the idea of one spirit, four souls. The explanation for that is quite complicated, and is shown in the following diagram:

Systematic table of *ichirei shikon*

The systematic table of one spirit (*ichirei*), four souls (*shikon*) in the hierarchy of Kami according to *Kojiki* and *Nihonshoki*:

FOUR SOULS AND ONE SPIRIT	NAME OF KAMI	EXPLANATION
naohinomitama	① *Amenominakanushi no kami*	Central Kami for everything, that is, the entire circle of the universe.
kushimitama & aramitama	② *Takamimusubi no kami*	Positive action—the source of all exterior manifestation.
nigimitama & sachimitama	③ *Kamimusubi no kami*	Negative action, the source of all inner, interior phenomena.
aramitama	④ *Umashiashikabihikoji no kami*	The generating energy of heaven which descends to earth.
nigimitama	⑤ *Amenotokotachi no kami*	Place for expressions in heaven.

These Kami are the first "five Kami of heaven," separated from all other Kami in rank.

The Kami with the numbers ④ and ⑤ unite heaven and earth with the two following Kami:

kushimitama	⑥ *Kuninotokotachi no kami*	Place for expressions on earth.
sachimitama	⑦ *Toyokumono no kami*	The generating energy of earth which ascends to heaven.

Through the combined effort of these four Kami (④, ⑤, ⑥, and ⑦) heaven and earth work upon each other.

kushimitama	⑧ *Uijini no kami* ⑨ *Suijini no kami*	
sachimitama	⑩ *Tsunugui no kami* ⑪ *Ikugui no kami*	These eight Kami are involved in the completion of earthly lives.
nigimitama	⑫ *Outonoji no kami* ⑬ *Outonobe no kami*	
aramitama	⑭ *Omodaru no kami* ⑮ *Ayakashikone no kami*	

These last eight Kami above are involved in the completion of earthly lives. Their appearance explains how earth formation is achieved and provides an explanation about how life on earth affects the earth. These last ten Kami (numbers ⑥–⑮) are the "Kami of earth."

naohinomitama (ichirei)		These two Kami are the earthly creators, in contrast to the heavenly creators. That is, they are the children given birth by Kami of heaven and who have become parents on earth. They are the first descendants from heaven.
kushimitama & aramitama	⑯ *Izanagi no kami*	
nigimitama & sachimitama	⑰ *Izanami no kami*	

Kami from *Kunitokotachi no kami* to *Izanagi* and *Izanami* represent seven generations of the Kami era.

naohinomitama	⑱ *Izanagi no omikami*	After *misogi* this Kami raised his status and advanced to the rank of *Amenominakanushi no kami.*
naohinomitama	⑲ *Amaterasu omikami*	This Kami is the manifestation of *Amenominakanushi no kami.*

The spirit of Kami also has four souls. At the shrine, usually *nigimitama* is enshrined in the main- or inner-shrine called *honden*, and *aramitama* is installed in the shrine called *Oku no miya* which is located at the back of the main shrine, or enshrined in a separate place.

This resembles the custom of placing human bones of the dead in the tomb (this bone is the symbol of *aramitama*) and the enshrinement of the spirit (*nigimitama*) on the mortuary tablet (*ihai*). For in Japan after a person dies, they are given another name and this is written on a tablet that the surviving family uses as an object for prayer.

Sachimitama, *kushimitama* and *naohinomitama*, each of which is the spirit of that Kami, reside in *Takamanohara*, which is above and beyond this world. Therefore during special festival services it is necessary for us to ask for their descent to be present here and to worship each of these three. To practice this service, we need to sincerely purify the priest and the believer as well as the shrine and *kamizane*. *Kamizane* is a physical representation of Kami such as a mirror in a main shrine (see Chapter 3).

It is understood that the idea of one spirit, four souls is inherent in all things. With minerals, *aramitama* is the predominant influence, whilst with plant and animal life *nigimitama* is foremost. As an example, I will present here the plant case as follows:

ICHIREI SHIKON OF TREE

aramitama	The work of the form of the tree, and represents the wooden nature of the tree.
nigimitama	Represents the sap and resin of the tree.
sachimitama	The work of the generative organs of the tree—blooming flowers and bringing fruit.
kushimitama	This is the vitality of the tree's growth, and the work of expressing the character of the tree.

ICHIREI SHIKON OF HUMAN BEING

aramitama	Governs every organ of the physical body such as the bone, muscle, intestine, etc.
nigimitama	Governs the blood, body fluid, lymphatic fluid, skin, hair, brain, eyeballs, etc.
sachimitama	Balances the body fluids and hormones, the function of sexual desire, senses, and so on, as well as generative energy.
kushimitama	Governs human life. This is the force for generating and transforming human beings through nerves, etc.

functions of body and mind	Bodily functions, governed by *aramitama* and *nigimitama*.	Emotional, mental, and spiritual aspects, governed by *sachimitama* and *kushimitama*.
aramitama	Renewal operations and metabolic operations.	Emotional operation of rigidity and hardening of the mind/heart. Destructive consciousness. Desire of materialistic expression.
nigimitama	Monitors the operation of nerves and muscles, and excites and calms.	Emotional operation of flexibility. The emotion of stagnation as well as driving desire—the emotion of feeling and touching.
sachimitama	Controls the faculty of the senses and reproductive organs, and balances the physical body.	The senses, passion, love, harmonious consciousness, desire to study or inquiry.

kushimitama	The operation of life energy, which incorporates and integrates external stimuli and mental events, renovating and transforming.	The desire to seek mystery, desire for creative contemplation, the ability of intuition and apperception.

This idea that there is a spiritual hierarchy contained in the human person is also to be found in the modern mysticism of the West. For example, both the school of Theosophy founded by Madame Blavatsky (1831–91) and the school of Anthroposophy founded by Rudolf Steiner (1861–1925) explain that human bodies exist at the following levels: 1) Physical body, 2) Etheric body, 3) Astral body, 4) Mental body, 5) Causal body.

Spiritualism, which flourished in America and England in the 19th century, also incorporated this hierarchy: 1) Physical body, 2) Body-double, 3) Etheric body, 4) Subtle body, and 5) Light body.

If we try to make a concordance between the concepts of Western mysticism and *ichirei shikon*, it could be done in the following way:

ICHIREI SHIKON	THEOSOPHY	SPIRITUALISM
1. *aramitama*	Physical body	Physical body
2. Between *ara* and *nigi*	Etheric body	Body Double
3. *nigimitama*	Astral body	Etheric body
4. *sachimitama*	Mental body	Subtle body
5. *kushimitama*	Causal body	Light body

There is also the traditional Chinese idea of two components of the human soul: *kon* and *haku*. We can think of the first as corresponding to *kushimitama* and *sachimitama* and the second one to *nigimitama* and *aramitama*. It should be noted here that this theory of *shikon* comes from the ancient idea of four elements, so there is the theory that corresponds earth to *aramitama*, water to *nigimitama*, fire to *sachimitama*, and air to *kushimitama*.

The function of *shikon*

When *shikon* in a human being becomes either too strong or too weak, that person loses his or her natural balance. An imbalance of *shikon* results in physical illness, psychological symptoms, personality disorders, or simply behavior that is said to be "out of character." Here I shall give an overview of the working of each *mitama*, indicating both its positive qualities and the effects on the individual if its workings are too weak or too strong.

kushimitama

When a person has this quality in abundance, he or she will possess intuitive ability and a strong spiritual sense, along with practical wisdom and the capacity for self-regulation. He or she will think along intelligent lines, be rich in spirit and also achieve physical equilibrium. A person with a balanced *kushimitama* can attain mystical powers and use them wisely. He or she can experience apperception and travel to or communicate with the upper-level worlds.

If *kushimitama* functions too strongly, however, it can induce hypersensitivity or even psychosis. The function of the liver or spleen can become overly sensitive and easily excited, and conditions such as diabetes and high blood pressure can arise. Physical exercise can help us avoid an over-abundance of *kushimitama*.

If *kushimitama* is weak, there is a loss of willpower and the capacity for coherent thought and action. Self-perception is reduced, and there are risks of neurasthenic conditions or amnesia. A weak *kushimitama* is often reflected in a facial expression that lacks energy, a demeanor characterized by lack of emotion and aridity or meanness of spirit. Recovering from this deficiency is more a psychological than a physical process. It involves the development of the mind, through intense concentration, and the cultivation of a mentality of gratitude, openness, and generosity of spirit.

sachimitama

An abundance of this quality leads to emotional riches and acute sensibility, resulting in an artistic temperament and interests. The person with abundant *sachimitama* will make a favorable impression on others and is likely to have refined and elegant taste.

When *sachimitama* is too strong, the affected person tends to become temperamental or even hysterical. He or she will be driven by passing fancies or transient passions, and will become self-indulgent and lustful.

When *sachimitama* becomes too weak, there is a loss of sensibility, an inability to feel or be moved by anything, and a mood of inertia, giving rise to indolence, lethargy, depression, and insecurity.

Sachimitama is sometimes written as *sakihi mitama*. The word *sachi* means "happiness," while *saki* means "living" or "alive." The confluence of these words in *sachi/sakihi mitama* shows that this *mitama* is closely associated with the source of life energy.

To keep *sachimitama* at a balanced level, one needs to develop a good and satisfying social life, based on loving and caring relationships with other people.

nigimitama

An abundance of this quality is good for the endocrine system and produces good physical health reflected in a lithe, youthful appearance and, in particular, healthy skin. A balanced *nigimitama* creates a calm, magnanimous temperament and a broad-minded, tolerant attitude to life.

When *nigimitama* becomes too strong, the affected person tends to overwork or indulge in an intemperate lifestyle. He or she becomes too sensitive and is easily influenced by evil thoughts, malice, or bad vibrations from other people.

When *nigimitama* is too weak, the affected person ages prematurely in mind, body, and spirit.

aramitama

An abundance of this quality leads to an active metabolism and healthy bones and muscles. It is likely to stimulate a person's athletic interests and prowess, and along with a strong will and increased energy and vitality. It also happens that people with a strong element of *aramitama* tend to lose their more graceful manners and assume at times a wild and combative air. This should not be seen as negative in itself, since they share such characteristics with the Kami of Izumo, *Onamuchi no kami*, who used them in a positive way.

Too much *aramitama* leads to a loss of both reason and sensitivity. It triggers a more than normal increase of sexual desire, egotism, and rudeness.

When *aramitama* is weak, the result is physical sickliness and a weakening of the muscles and bones. The affected person loses the desire to be active, physically or mentally, and becomes weak-willed. Negative emotions prevail, so that the person comes to regard all activity as troublesome and taxing, and becomes a habitual complainer. Also, the affected person displays a tendency to tell lies without shame.

Many types of illness, mental and physical, are created by imbalances of the *shikon*, or four souls. Yamakage Shinto has an esoteric tradition of medicine, a process of healing based on the rebalancing of the four souls. That knowledge, however, is the subject of another book.

The spiritual structure of human beings

Human beings can be seen as having four aspects: physical, emotional, intellectual, and spiritual. These aspects correspond with the four souls in the structure of *ichirei shikon* (one spirit, four souls). However, we should not presume that for all human beings this structure of one spirit, four souls is for everybody one and the same. This structure is for every individual a different one.

According to the tradition of Yamakage Shinto, our universe (or the big circle of the universe) is a current of whirling spirits springing out of *daigenrei* (great original spirit). In this spiritual current individuals with their own identity are generated, like sparks of energy, which are also manifested as a vortex. The energies of *aramitama* and *nigimitama*, operating on an unconscious level, cooperate within these entities in order to generate matter. Next on a conscious level the energies of *kushimitama* and *sachimitama* make life appear by joining in the processes initiated by *aramitama* and *nigimitama*.

Human beings are seen as an assemblage of 350 to 500 of these sparks of energy. Finally the human being comes into existence, when *naohinomitama* (which is the same as *ichirei*, meaning one spirit) descends onto this collection of energy particles. In the same pre-scientific tradition it is said that when a total of 100 to 300 of these energy sparks come together, this will mean the creation of higher-ranked animals. From 50 to 100 will create lower animals; fewer than 50 will create plants, and fewer than 30 will create minerals. Some human beings can project their *bunrei* (*wakemitama*)—a part of their own spirit—to a different place. This is possible because human beings are the collective sum of many souls or *mitama*.

When human beings die, their one spirit, *naohinomitama* and two of the four souls, *kushimitama* and *sachimitama* go to the other world, while the other two souls, *nigimitama* and *aramitama* remain on earth. They stay there for a while, but eventually they can disappear. Ideally they can be purified to join *kushimitama* or *sachimitama*. This idea corresponds to the Chinese philosophy of Daoist hermits with supernatural powers. The higher part of the human soul or *tama* goes up to heaven, and the lower part, or *paku* (*haku*), goes back to the earth. Here we note a significant difference between the structure of one spirit, four souls of *koshinto* and the Chinese concept, which is based upon the dual layered *konpaku*, where *kon* is the higher part and *paku* or *haku* is the lower part of the soul.

Death and the theory of four souls

With death, *naohinomitama*, *kushimitama*, and *sachimitama* leave the human body, and *nigimitama* and *aramitama* remain here in this world.

Aramitama governs the physical body, so it disintegrates either with decomposition if buried in the earth or with burning if it is cremated. Also, negative energy is emitted with the disintegration of the dead body (*aramitama*) and this explains the "uncleanness of death" (*kegare*).

Nigimitama also goes through a disintegration process, but it sometimes takes more time. One part of *nigimitama* remains in this world to become the base for contact between this physical world and the lower astral world, or *yukai*. Therefore in a memorial service for an ancestor, the *nigimitama* is the object of worship. So the soul that is attached to the memorial tablet is actually this *nigimitama*.

In the "divine celebration words for building up the Izumo nation," it is stated that *Okuninushi no mikoto* made the following order to be performed after his death:

"Project my *nigimitama* to *yatano kagami* and call it *Yamato no omono-nushi kushimikatama no mikoto* and enshrine it at *kannabi* in Yamato."

In this way, worshipping *nigimitama* as the way for worshipping the spirit of the dead is described. *Yatano kagami* is the mirror and one of the three Imperial Regalia.

In the words used at the ancient Yamakage Shinto funeral service there is a saying that, "as for the corpse, we respectfully return it to the original great earth of coarse mineral. As for *nigimitama*, it remains in this world for a long time. And as for *kushimitama* and *sachimitama*, we respectfully let them ascend to the high throne of the other world."

In the case of an unexpected death, such as death in a car accident, *aramitama* and a part of *nigimitama* of the victim remain in the site of the accident. That place often carries a feeling of attachment, or a grudge or bitterness of the dead person. This feeling can be activated and sensed by any psychic approaching there. The psychic researcher calls the spirit in this condition "the spirit chained to earth." This type of spirit in most cases is not the real body of the spirit-soul (*reikon*), but rather like the remaining ether (*zanki*), if I dare to name it. If this ether is strong, there will be the phenomenon of a ghostly apparition. In such a situation, everything will be restored to normal, if we apply an appropriate process of purification.

In general, *naohinomitama*, *kushimitama*, and *sachimitama* move on to the other world, but they do not necessarily go straight to the higher World of Kami (*shinkai*). If we can ever talk of *naohinomitama* only, *naohinomitama* as its own nature can go straight to the world of Kami since it is pure and bright without any uncleanness. But *kushimitama* and *sachimitama*, which are attached to *naohinomitama*, have some impurity, so *naohinomitama* can float only half way to the higher world.

Kushimitama is concerned with the function of thinking and integrating, so it is really wisdom or reason itself. Since *kushimitama* still has some impurity, that is to say some heaviness, one cannot gain a cheerful clarity and brightness (*seimei*) without purifying one's thoughts and knowledge.

Sachimitama is concerned with the function of love and sentiment, so here again one cannot gain the clarity and brightness without purification of sentiments and feelings through experience. When these two remain impure, they pull down *naohinomitama*.

Therefore, midway to the higher world of Kami, one works on one's own purification to clear sentiments and thoughts in order to be able to eventually advance to that higher, spiritual world.

In the period immediately after death, the spirit-soul remains close to this world, observing how the family is doing, going out to visit friends at their home, or going to worship at a shrine or Buddhist temple. Many are not yet clearly aware of their own death status. Some still retain a part of *nigimitama*, so they have a semi-material body and can even make noises. Those who have psychic powers are able to see them. Usually they spend a certain period of time, the so-called "forty-nine days," in such circumstances. In Buddhism they call this circumstance *chuyu*, meaning "existing in the middle." A while afterwards they become aware of their death and fully move onto the other world, or *yukai*.

CHAPTER 7

Koshinto

View of the "Other World"

Where do human beings go after death?

Modern science and materialism both point toward the idea that human beings exist only at the physical level and so there is no such thing as life after death. They are extremely reluctant to accept the validity of any evidence for the existence of another world. Those who have spiritual or religious beliefs have tried to convince secular scientists and philosophers of the reality of existence beyond the mundane, but often they seem to be operating in parallel intellectual universes that cannot overlap. However, no matter how much people negate the existence of the world after death, they cannot make it disappear.

Even in spiritual circles, those who are deeply immersed in modern academic approaches tend to despise, or at least be highly skeptical about, all mystical experience. Those who are not trained in esoteric discipline flatly negate mystical and spiritual experience. They merely state that "going to the pure land after death" and "being saved by Buddha or Bodhisattva" are just expressions of people's inner beliefs, and do not actually exist. I doubt that people can really be satisfied with that understanding and fully accept it.

At the other extreme, there are some who, suspending their critical faculties, completely believe the sayings of low-level psychics. Such people are trapped in a belief that the world after death is filled with only wicked or evil spirits. This is because they do not know that psychics at a low level only respond to spirits at that same low level.

Since ancient times, Shinto has taught that the goal of human life is to "become like a Kami" through the work of refining the personality and bringing out a clean and bright character. This work is understood to continue even after death. For beyond death, there is a high and pure world as well as a low and unclean one. Therefore, every spirit-soul (*reikon*) has to continue training for purification and further spiritual advancement even after physical death. This is the hidden knowledge gained by the experience of Shinto practitioners over its long history.

In Yamakage Shinto we can find the following "Song of the Spiritual Journey":

Tokoshie ni	As long as I am here
Onore no aran	the road to purify
Kagiri ni wa	my spirit-soul
Mitama Kiyome no	will never end
Michi wa tayumaji	

Ancient views of the world after death

Ancient Japanese have expressed the world after death in various ways. Beyond death, one is said to go to the following variously expressed realms:

the eternal land, or the land of root

(*tokoyonokuni*, or *nenokuni*)

the hidden world (astral world) (*kakuriyo*)

the land of the dead (Hades) (*yominokuni*)

the mountain, where the dead become guardian Kami, watching over their family for generations to come.

The eternal land and the land of root are mentioned in the *Kojiki*, *Nihonshoki*, and *Man'yoshu*. It is the place where the soul-spirit (*reikon*) receives eternal life, and the place where every new life is generated. It is therefore also referred to as the "land of mother."

In the section of the *Kojiki* dedicated to the Kami *Susanoo no mikoto*, there is the saying, "I am going to go to the land of mother, the *katasu* land of root (*nenokatasukuni*)." "Root" (*ne*) implies the source that gives birth to everything. "The eternal world" (*tokoyo*) implies the land full of life energy where eternal youth is maintained. In volume 4 of the *Man'yoshu*, a collection of ancient Japanese short songs, there is a song with the words, "my wife must have lived in the land of the eternal world; she has become younger than when I saw her in the past."

Apparently the ancient Japanese had the image of "the land of the eternal world" as a place far across the ocean. In the section on Emperor Jimmu in volume 2 of the *Kojiki*, there is a saying, "*Mikenu no mikoto* (another name for Jimmu) has gone to the land of the eternal world by walking on the wave." In the section on Emperor Suinin, there is also a saying, "Ise is the land where the waves of the eternal world go back and forth." This was said by *Amaterasu omikami* when she settled down in the land of Ise.

In the story of *Umisachihiko* and *Yamasachihiko* (the names of two young men, one living in the mountains, the other near the ocean), there is an episode where a mountain man, *Yamasachihiko*, visits the palace of the ocean Kami. There is also a dragon castle in the story of Taro Urashima, and all these include similar imagery of the ocean in the eternal land.

In Okinawa, it is also said that the land of Kami, called *niraikanai*, exists far away across the ocean. This belief was later influenced by Buddhism and developed into the belief in the pure land of Fudaraku. In Kumano, in order to attain Nirvana, the believer at the end of his life could practice "crossing the ocean toward Fudaraku" by rowing a small boat into the southern sea.[14] The reason for the emphasis on the south lies in the popular Buddhist teaching that the palace of the dragon Kami is located in Sri Lanka. This was said to be the pure land of Fudaraku, because Sri Lanka is located in the southern ocean, beyond the Indian subcontinent.

The word *kakuriyo* (the hidden world) does not appear in the ancient literature. However, the provenance of the word is also ancient, and denotes an invisible world that contrasts to the known or visible world (*utsushiyo*). After all, the entire universe is the land of Kami, and the ancients viewed the universe as consisting of both visible and invisible worlds. According to the teaching handed down to Yamakage Shinto, our material world mirrors the hidden world, and every existence is the mirrored embodiment of the spirit of Kami, or *shinrei*. Therefore we can say that the hidden world is the land of root (*nenokuni*), that is, the root from which everything has emerged.

As for the word *yominokuni* (Hades), there is a strong sense of continental Asian origin. Its literal meaning is the "underworld for the dead." There is a very famous episode of a visit to Hades by *Izanagi no mikoto* in the *Kojiki*. This word, *yominokuni*, seems to have been influenced by Chinese Taoism. In ancient China, we find deep underground tombs, and in Okinawa there are also cave burial customs that suggest consciousness of a world below. This notion of an underground world is colored with a strong sense of the uncleanness of death. It is at variance with most other Japanese conceptions of the other world.

The view of the other world expressed by the idea of the mountain is well established and broadly accepted by the Japanese. Songs in the *Man'yoshu* refer to a place called "Hase in Yamato" which is a spiritual world after death. There are several more places like these, such as Mt. Myochi (*Myochi san*) in Nachi, Mt. Haku (*Haku san*) in Kaga, Mt. Gastsu (*Gassan*) in Dewa, Mt. Tate (*Tate yama*), Mt. Osore (*Osore zan*) in Mutsu, among others. These mountains are called spiritual mountains in Japan, and they used to be sacred places to which it was thought the spirits of dead human beings went. These spiritual mountains also became the base for the school of mountain ascetics that has existed since the arrival of Buddhism in Japan. According to Japanese folklore, the spirits of the dead remain for a certain time at the mountain to watch over their descendants and to receive memorial services. After being completely purified, the spirit stays within the mountain, but moves to a higher dimension to become one of the ancestral spirits of that village.

In some places, people used to believe that in January these ancestral spirits came down from the mountain to become Kami for the rice field in order to bring a good harvest. After the harvest festival in autumn, the spirits went back to the mountain to become mountain Kami again in order to protect their posterity. This belief also exists in Okinawa, and they call the mountain at the back of the village "Kushatenoutaki."

Therefore, it has been widely believed in Japan that ancestral spirits exist in the invisible world, overlapping with physical reality and having intimate connection with people living in this world. In this unseen world, the ancestral spirits continue to work on their own purification.

It was also widely believed that having completed some degree of purification, the spirits would move on to a higher level of the "world of spirits of Kami" (*shinreikai*). This purification process is thought to be very much the same as the process of inner growth for people living in the contemporary material world.

Therefore, the structure of the memorial service at each special anniversary for the dead was a replica of the ritual service for each important turning point of inner growth during our life here on earth.

There is also another myth of humans going straight to *Takamano-hara*—the highest level of the world of Kami after death. However this was originally presented as a joke in order to counter Buddhist influence. In reality, the Japanese did not seriously believe that human beings could immediately enter *Takamanohara*, even though there are some human spirit-souls which join with Kami after becoming a focus for devotion, that is to say a noble spirit-Kami (*reijin*). They achieve this status through great work during their lives in this world. *Taka-manohara*, however, is thought to be of such a high order that no spirit-souls could easily be accepted to that level, no matter how hard and for how long they have worked on their purification. In this context, it is important to be aware that *reijin* (spirit-Kami) is different from *shinrei* (spirit of Kami). The former is the spirit who has reached the rank of Kami through spiritual work, while the latter is the essence or nature of Kami that descends.

Today, the early Japanese view of the other worlds for the dead is widely described as a horizontal theory. This means that it conceived of the other world as "beyond the ocean" or as "the inner mountain," realms parallel to the material world rather than above or beyond it. It was during the *Kofun* era (ca. 300–710; known as the "era of the ancient tomb"), that the "vertical" view of other worlds of the dead reached Japan from the Asian mainland. The Buddhist view of the world of heaven for the dead also spread to Japan at around this time. With the exception of the unique episode of the visit to Hades by

Izanagi no mikoto, the ancient Japanese believed that human beings continue living in the other world after death. Their life there is quite similar to the one here, even though the other world is more bright and lucid in character.

This concept is different from both the Buddhist idea of the pure land and the Christian notion of heaven. Even in *Takamanohara*, the highest level of the world of Kami, each Kami works and strives. In the *Kojiki* and *Nihonshoki*, there are descriptions of labors in the rice field, the farming of silk worms, weaving, rituals and worship, and the work of the blacksmith. Those two books explain that these labors are archetypal representations of the work of humanity.

The spirit-soul's journey

Gradually, each human spirit-soul is purified so that it may become a highly advanced spirit, just as flowers bloom, bring forth fruit, and eventually mature. The soul who committed misdeeds undergoes a process of atonement. Having successfully worked through this, it is able to move on to further spiritual growth. Some very advanced psychics are conscious of this process taking place.

The festival for ancestral spirits, or annual memorial service, should be performed with an understanding of the process of spiritual growth. Ancestral spirits can ascend to the rank of spirit-guide for their descendants only by going through their own purification process. So that ancestors may be able to protect and guide their descendants, they need

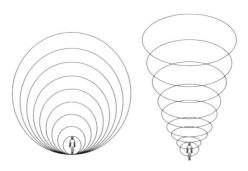

The process of spiritual advancement

the prayers of living people who have a proper spiritual awareness. This involves understanding that the spiritual path and the quest for purification continue for human beings even after they are physically dead. The realms that humans go to after death can range from those of the higher level of the world of Kami all the way down to the hidden world of *yukai*, which literally means "lower astral world," a level closer to our own. Spirit-souls undergo rigorous training after death and receive instructions from the higher world, which can be difficult and demanding. In our present physical realm, we should begin with the understanding that we are spiritually immature and seek to advance gradually to a higher status by the training of the mind and the purification of the spirit-soul.

In the ancient tradition of Yamakage Shinto, the process of spiritual advancement is presented in the form of nine circles (see figure). For a deeper understanding of this spiritual journey after death Yamakage Shinto has also developed the theory of one spirit, four souls. This supports the daily practice of purification training, as understood by practitioners of Yamakage Shinto. An outline of this theory can be found in Chapter 6. In this section, death and the life beyond it is explained in the terms of one spirit, four souls.

The spirits of Kami protect the dead during the transition to the other world (*yukai*)

During the period of transition from this world to *yukai*, the hidden world of subtle energy, the spirit-soul is at its most vulnerable. It can be likened to a delicate butterfly, at the moment of emergence from its chrysalis. Therefore, there are spirits entrusted with the task of protecting the spirit-soul from danger at this time.

In most cases, the spirits of deceased ancestors or friends of the dead come to meet and greet the dead. These spirits in turn receive instruction from higher ranks of spirit so that they may give useful guidance to their dead relatives or friends. In Japan, the spirit of Kami (*shinrei*) of the *ubusuna jinja*, or local shrine, protects each locality and usually assumes the role of this higher-ranking spirit. Those who are spiritually aware will be sure to enjoy the protection of the spirit-guide that emanates from that local shrine, and this spirit will help them through their transition to the other world.

However, even for those who derive benefit from the spirit-guide, it

157

is necessary to conduct the funeral ceremony at the local shrine. This is where the spirit of Kami sits, assuming a role akin to the governing officer of Hades. Wherever it is held, a Shinto funeral service always involves the ritual of "informing" the *ubusuna jinja*. Even if the funeral service is held in accordance with a different religious or spiritual tradition, the death should be reported to the local shrine.

Protected by the spirit-guide, the dead person prepares for the transition to *yukai*, the other world. He or she enters the life in the other world after being given various instructions and help. In the case of a person suddenly dying in an accident, for example, that person will probably not be aware of his or her death. In this situation, the spirit-guide gives kind support to that person and escorts his or her spirit to the other world.

It is often asked what happens after death to those who have committed evil deeds, or who can be described as truly evil in their conduct and attitude. Their spirit-souls are impure and cloudy, releasing unclean vibrations, and so they gather together at dark, cloudy places that reflect their inner state. They are dragged into the world of illusion, delusion, and suffering, which is the only appropriate place for such spirits. However, it is very rare to find this kind of contaminated spirit. Most people eventually move to *yukai*, even if they have to go through a process of temporary atonement for purification.

Here it is important to be aware that this other world, *yukai*, is not the world of the higher spirits. Rather, it is the spiritual equivalent of a beautiful flower garden. In certain schools of Japanese Buddhism, this concept also exists and is called *gokuraku jodo*, the pure land of paradise. However this is conceived of as a place of non-action, whereas in the other world of Shinto, spirits can be actively engaged in a wide range of projects.

Why do *kannushi* not perform the funeral at the Shinto shrine?

Many Japanese visit Shinto shrines for devotional purposes and yet have their funerals held at Buddhist temples. In recent years, Christian-style weddings have become fashionable, making the situation even more complicated. Many Western observers find Japanese spiritual practices hard to disentangle and so are tempted to dismiss Japanese spirituality as convoluted and confused. In their own terms of reference, they are quite right. Japanese spiritual practice is complex and subtle, and so it is hard to classify according to Western concepts of "either/or." This is a strength in many respects. However, it must also be said that in Japan, as in other advanced industrial societies, a climate of spiritual ignorance has arisen. This leads, among other things, to a casual, "mix and match" approach to spiritual practice. Therefore, those who move randomly from one practice to another—a Christian wedding to a Buddhist funeral, for instance—often justify themselves by saying that the marriage and funeral ceremonies are only customs.

From earliest times, we have not conducted funeral services at

Shinto shrines. This does not necessarily mean that we have never had Shinto funeral services as such, but even when we did, we never used the shrine for the funeral location. That is the case even with the funeral of the shrine's *kannushi*.

There are several reasons for this. To begin with, the shrine is a clean and pure place where the spirit of Kami descends. It is therefore not the place to bring a powerful uncleanness such as that of a dead body. This has been understood in Japan from ancient times. Instead, a night of vigil takes place at the dead person's home, and after a farewell service the body is buried at a burial site. The Shinto shrine is not involved in this process.

When Buddhism first arrived in Japan, the Buddhist temple assumed the task of conducting memorial services for the dead, and so has been strongly involved in funeral rites since medieval times. Through the Tokugawa government's enforcement of "the parishioner system in the Buddhist temple," each family developed a supporting relationship with a particular temple of their choice, to whose care they entrusted the funeral, the ashes of the dead, and the positioning of the tomb. Thus Shinto abandoned the funeral service duty, except in some areas of Japan where Buddhist influences were slower to penetrate.

Since the Meiji era (1868–1912), however, there has been a ceremony called a "Shinto funeral," but it is not conducted by a *kannushi*. Instead, it is carried out by the teacher of a particular Shinto group called Kyoha Shinto. This is not ancient Shinto, but is made up of several schools that have a founder, doctrine, teacher, and a meeting place for teaching. We cannot therefore claim that this post-Meiji funeral service is conducted in accordance with *koshinto*.

Originally, funeral services and marriage ceremonies took place in a family or community setting. The corpse was also supposed to be buried at an appropriate place within the community. During the Edo period (1600–1867), however, it became the general practice for Buddhist temples to be asked to care for the cremated ashes of the dead. Therefore, the recent trend in Japan toward public cemeteries and the vogue for natural burial services without formal religious affiliation can both be seen as a return to ancient ways of disposing of the dead.

In Shinto, a corpse is seen as merely a shell without a spirit-soul, and so it should not be the object of special veneration. Instead, it is considered as somewhat unclean, and so it has to be disposed of quite rapidly. Villages used to have what was known as a "cemetery for burying or throwing away," but in the mid-1960s the Japanese government prohibited internment there on health grounds, because of concerns over disease epidemics. We can find the ruins of this type of cemetery throughout Japan, a place that was used literally to throw away the corpse. The corpse itself is not important; what matters is where the spirit-soul has gone.

The uncleanness of death is caused by the negative energy released during the disintegration of the physical body, *aramitama* and *nigimitama*. Recently, scholars of ethnic customs and folklore have researched and explained the triad structure of *hare, ke, and kegare*. According to this model, *kegare* is interpreted as *ke* (*chi* or *ki* energy)—*gare* (withers or leaves). They also present the relationship between *hare* and *kegare* as people transforming the energy of uncleanness (*kegare*) into clean energy through a purification exercise (*harai*). However, this explanation can only be seen as an abstract and therefore incomplete academic approach from the viewpoint of spiritual practitioners. *Kegare* emitted either during the disintegration of the body or from wicked thoughts has a semi-material power, and so we purify it only by washing it away or burning it out. We cannot transform the malignant energy into good; therefore we should avoid contact with it as much as we can. Purification has to be carried out thoroughly and according to strict principles, and so the corpse cannot be introduced into the sacred space.

From a spiritual perspective, reverence for a corpse or cremated ashes is ultimately meaningless. The real memorial service for the spirit of the dead is a process of talking to the dead to convince them to move on to a higher spiritual plane. It is also about praying to the higher spirit of Kami to guide the new spirit. We can practice this service away from the place where a corpse or the ashes are held or where the tomb is established. It is helpful to use a memorial tablet, to which the *nigimitama* of the deceased person will be attracted (see also Chapter 6). Japanese families often prepare such tablets and offer prayers in front of them every day at their home altar, but even these procedures are not strictly necessary. Not only is it meaningless but it is also positively dangerous to go to the unclean (*kegare*) place of the corpse or ashes. We should not confuse the idea of a clean inner circle with that of a cemetery for throwing away a corpse.

It should be noted that the spirit of the dead sometimes stays around in the early stages, but usually the spirit moves quickly into the other world. It rarely comes down to the tomb or to a funeral hall. Needless to say the impurity (*kegare*) of the corpse has to be expunged. It is also necessary to drive away the evil spirit or *magatsubi*, which tries to get into the corpse, and purify the family members who were exposed to the unclean energy from the dead. This purification practice can be done either by a Shinto *kannushi* or Buddhist monk with well-developed spiritual powers.

My own belief is that the real reason why *kannushi* during the Edo period were so willing to let Buddhist monks take care of the dead was that they did not wish to come into contact with the uncleanness. Where a *kannushi* did take care of the funeral service for a colleague, he would avoid any service at a shrine for an entire month. This was both because he was in mourning and because he had to undergo a restrictive cleansing process himself.

What is the memorial service for the dead?

The memorial service for honoring the dead involves praying for the spirit of the dead to be able to advance into a higher world. These prayers are not aimed indiscriminately at all participating spirits, but at the governing Kami of the other world, who is asked to provide good instructions to the new spirit. The memorial service to grieve for the passing of the dead may be for the comfort and solace of the family here on earth, but it has no spiritual meaning.

To what form of governing Kami do we pray in Shinto? It is a Kami known to the world as *Okuninushi no mikoto* who resides in the Izumo Shrine. We appeal to him for protection, addressing him in this instance by the title *Kakuriyo oshiro shimesu okami* (The Great Kami Governing the Hidden World). His status is that of head of all local Kami (*Sobusuna kami*), and so he administers and watches over all living people as well as the dead. He assumed this role when he vowed, "I shall govern the matter of the hidden world since I am going to retire there." This occurred at the time he "gave up the governorship of this (material) world."

There are also instances in which we seek help and instruction from some of our own ancestors who worked hard to purify and advance to the higher level and so increase their spiritual power. At that higher level, such ancestors are chosen as a higher spirit to help common spirits. Their high status was acquired through hard work and training in the hidden world (*yukai*) or the world of spirit (*reikai*). It need not be related in any way to high status in society or an accumulation of knowledge through study during their lives in this world. The more of these types of spirit we have among our ancestral spirits, the more protection we are able to draw upon. For this reason, it is very important for us to honor our ancestors and offer prayers on their behalf.

CHAPTER 8

The Systematic Training
Method of *Chinkon*

The Kami within

All human beings have the potential to become Kami.

Within every human being there resides *naohinomitama*, which, literally translated from the written characters, means "spirit of straight fire or sun." This *naohinomitama* is *wakemitama* (or *bunrei*) of *daigenrei* (the great original spirit). That is, *wakemitama* is a child-spirit of *daigenrei*, the Creator Kami of the universe. This *naohinomitama* is pure and has great wisdom.

A song (*goshinka*) in Yamakage Shinto says:

Ame tsuchi wo	From the creating spirit
Tsukuri tamaeshi	of heaven and earth
Mioya yori	I have received the soul
Mitama wo ukeshi	by which I am who I am.
Ware koso ware wa	

However, we can lose touch with this *naohinomitama* through our involvement in daily, mundane affairs. The four souls (*shikon*) surrounding *naohinomitama* (see Chapter 6) become disturbed and unfocused, so the body and mind are anxious and fail to find calm. When

"Kami inside" does not manifest itself, a person cannot proceed upward on the path of renovating and maintaining and generating (or creating) and cultivating—the path that leads to self-realization as Kami.

This *naohinomitama* is also called the "true self" (*shinga*). Through worldly preoccupations, we become separated from that true self, and yet we can be aware that it exists and that it needs to get out. In a sense we can say that this phenomenon represents the separation between purity and impurity. To make this separation occur, a centrifugal separation movement of purity is needed. As a result of this movement, the true self, shrouded by the cloud of illusion and impurity, is able to emerge. The true self is a state of transcendence and so it is able to remain pure, even in the midst of impurity. However, the ego-self living in the relative and conflicted world cannot hear the voice of this true self. In order to hear this voice, we need to conduct silent listening in meditation. In Yamakage Shinto, that is known as *chinkon*.

When we carry out *chinkon*, the relationship between true self and ego-self does not have conflict, and they become one body like the front and back of one coin. This is known as the unification of Kami and the human being. This unification means that Kami and the human being spiritually become one.

Living in the flow of eternity

In Yamakage Shinto, there is a saying: "this body as it is, is Kami." This means that the human body itself, in its purely natural state, is

Kami. Within us resides *naohinomitama*, which is a child-spirit coming out of *daigenrei*, the great original spirit. All four souls, constituting "I" (see Chapter 6) and the material substance making up the physical body are also what *daigenrei* has created and made grown, transformed, and developed. When you see this reality in deep introspection through *chinkon* practice, you will intuitively know the truth of the saying, "this body as it is, is Kami." There is also the saying: "ancestors and 'I' are connected as one." This means the ancestors and "I" are connected with each other as one body.

"I" am one scene of an endless, continuous life history in the eternal universe. My ancestors who bore me are also the children of Kami, and they also received the same *naohinomitama* from *daigenrei* as I did. "I" have also inherited the physical body. "I" have inherited culture, knowledge and so on. A child-spirit (*wakemitama*) coming out of the same one spirit (*ichirei*), inherited by a present "I," keeps changing and moving toward Kami. This chronological process of birth, growth (becoming), transformation, development, that is, the creation process (*seisei kaiku*) is represented in the physical and spiritual succession within "I." Therefore, "'I' live" means 'I' am living in the flow of this eternity."

There is also the saying: "everything is 'I'." This means that everything is the result of the transformation and creation of *daigenrei*, the "creator Kami of the universe" and that the source of life is one. This also means everything that is manifest in that universe is interconnected, part of the web of life, from the most apparently complex organisms to the seemingly simplest. Any phenomenon manifested in "me" is meaningful and nurtures "me." In the end it moves "me" toward Kami. In this sense, every manifestation in the cosmos is a manifestation of "me."

All this should not be understood only at the rational level. It must be experienced intuitively as we access our inner Kami.

The meaning of *chinkon*

The word *chinkon*, also pronounced as *mitama shizume*, should not be confused with the practice of calming down the spirit of the dead. Also one should not think it is a kind of meditation in order to quiet the mind. There is a deeper meaning in the word. The word *chinkon* has a long history. It originates in a saying found in an article about *Iso no kami* Shrine in the old book named *Twenty-two Sha Hon'en*. This saying is:

"*Chinkon* means making our drifting soul settle down at *chufu* (*tanden*, the spot below the belly button)." In other words, it means finding the physical center and the center of consciousness.

In the book, *Ryoghi no Ge* (the interpretation of one of the old Law Orders issued in 718 A.D.) compiled in the Heian period, there is a saying:

> "We call people's cheerfulness (gaiety) *kon* (meaning *tama*, 'soul'). *Kon* is moving. We invite a drifting, moving soul (*kon*) to settle down at *chufu* (*tanden*). Therefore this

practice is called *chinkon*. *Chin* in this context means 'settle
or calm down,' *kon* means 'soul'."

The systematic method that is famous for this *chinkon* is the one
handed down at *Iso no kami* Shrine in Tenri city in Nara. They practice
this method by chanting mysterious spells called *Tokusa no kandakara*,
which means "the ten kinds of Kami's treasures." It has been considered
an ancient and secret method with which people can heal sickness or
even bring a dead person back to life by keeping the soul of the dead
from making the transition to the other world after physical death. This
method, by the way, is only used by Shinto priests to help people. It
is not a systematic method of spiritual training for seekers. Yamakage
Shinto has transmitted a different method of *Tokusa no kandakara*, but I
will not go into that here.

The soul of the typical person is scattered, drifting around the physical body without focusing at all. Bringing it together into a cohesive
state is the practice of *chinkon*. The desirable condition of the psyche/
mind is to have it condensed to the size of a soccer ball. The ideal condition is, if possible, 10 centimeters in diameter and positioned at *tanden*, right under the belly button. The process of bringing our mind
and psyche to this position is what we call *chinkon*. For it is only in this
condition that the mind becomes calm and the four souls (*shikon*) find
equilibrium. At this point, contact with the innermost *naohinomitama*
becomes possible. It is essential for people to have tools and methods,

such as the right way of sitting or breathing in order to reach this level. Many people appreciate the systematic method of training in Yamakage Shinto since it is easy and enjoyable for anyone to practice and to keep various processes in good balance.

The sequential order of *chinkon*

For full details of the practice, the reader should refer to Appendix 2. For now, I shall explore a few key themes, which are relevant to a wider understanding of Shinto.

First, we clean both the physical body and the mind/psyche through *misogi* practice. It is desirable that you take all your clothes off at the *misogi* place (bathroom) and take a cold shower. You first clean the groin area and next wash the eyes. Then you wash the inside of the mouth several times by holding large amounts of water in the mouth. Then wash the whole face and the ears. Next, wash the chest and the left shoulder down to the hand, and then do the same on the right side. You then wash the belly, the left thigh and foot, then the right thigh and foot. At the end you turn your back toward the shower. While getting the cold shower from the neck to the back, you chant the words for *misogi* purification—*misogi harai no kotoba* (see Appendix 2)—and clap the hands twice. It would be better still if you can use salt to clean the whole body. If circumstances do not allow you to go through this whole process, then wash the hands, rinse the mouth, and wash the entire face.

Sit directly facing the shrine, or *kamidana* (household altar) if practicing at home. Close your eyes and sit quietly for a while. Prepare the mind and then bow and clap the hands (two bows, two claps and one bow). Afterwards, read the "words for *misogi* purification" (*misogi harai no kotoba*) and the "words for great purification" (*oharai no kotoba*). All these recitations are voiced from the bottom of the belly with much energy gathered at the *tanden*, the spot right under the belly button. Read them respectfully, aiming at becoming totally free from any ideas and thoughts as you listen to your own voice.

After this, practice particular physical postures. There are two kinds of sitting methods in *chinkon* practice in Shinto—*seiza* and *anza*. The first, *seiza*, is sitting straight (formal) and the other, *anza*, is sitting at ease (informal). With the former, bend the knees leaving them about two fist lengths apart. Put one big toe upon the other, so they overlap. The latter informal posture is sitting cross-legged. Details such as whether or not a person should put their foot on the thigh are not that important. It is the best if the posture makes you feel secure, comfortable, and relaxed. However, it is vital that you hold your chest, neck, and head erect, and keep the spine stretched straight. To do this, it is a good idea to put a small cushion under your buttocks.

With eyes slightly open and looking up, try to look at the center of your forehead through the inside of the eyelids. As long as you do this, you will not see negative entities. However, if it is easier for you to focus on and practice the meditation with eyes closed, then close the eyes completely. Hands should be folded at the location of the *tanden*.

Although there is a formal posture for the hands, this may be transmitted only by oral instruction.

Dispersed mind and concentrated mind

Hand posture of *furutama*

The awakening of the soul (*furutama*)

The next step for the practitioner is the method of breathing within *chinkon*. To prepare for that, Yamakage Shinto provides another procedure called *furutama* (literal meaning: "shaking up the soul"). The *chinkon* method of "ten kinds of divine treasures" in the Isonokami Shrine is also called by another name: the "method of *furutama*." The shrine itself has been known as *furunoyashiro* (the Furu Shrine) since ancient times.

The chief priest of Isonokami Shrine, Master Takeo Mori once said:

> "One meaning of the word, *furutama*—sometimes also called *furitama*—is having spiritual strength (*miitsu*) poured down upon us by the spirit of Kami. 'Pour down upon' is *furisosogu* in Japanese. Another meaning is that we ourselves 'excite or energize our own spirit.'[15]
>
> In either case, we cannot receive much *mitamanofuyu*—'expanding *tama*-spirit'—if spiritual strength is not poured down upon us by the spirit of Kami."

As for the Yamakage Shinto method of *furitama* in *chinkon* practice, the point of exciting our own spirit by ourselves is emphasized.

First you either stand up or sit with legs crossed. Lace the fingers of both hands with only the index fingers stretched straight up together. Place that hand posture in front of your chest so that your hands are parallel to your chest. Spread out your elbows. Keeping that posture, gradually put energy into both arms and then lightly swing them.

Those who are spiritually receptive will start their hands moving automatically. The hands will shake intensely. It is in this state that one is being taken over by Kami (a state called *kamigakari*). We often find secular faith healers also doing it this way in order to be inspired and taken over by Kami.

This trembling movement soon spreads all over the whole body, without your own will, and the body begins automatically leaping, jumping, or forming strange postures. If you do this practice in a standing position, you might jump up 30 to 40 centimeters. Actually, you might jump up without changing your posture, even while sitting with legs crossed. Because of this, we avoid sitting in *seiza*, the formal way, since you might hurt the knees. Occasionally, some people utter strange sounds like certain animals, or they gesture like a bird flapping its wings.

For beginners, this kind of automatic movement may hardly occur. The person then needs to move his or her hands intentionally in order to rouse up this inner power. When the person feels his or her body wanting to move without will it should be allowed to happen. The person must let go of intention or a fear of being embarrassed and try to create this state of intense excitement.

You cannot sustain this kind of intense movement for a long time. After a minute or two, the heart will pound hard and breathing will be rough, and you will begin to feel unable to do this practice any longer. Allow the intensity of the whole body to slow down and loosen up. This process is called "absent-mindedness." At this point your agitated blood flow will calm down, your heart and mind will become quiet, and you will find your deep, calm place.

When you repeat this intense movement two or three times, your entire body perspires and your mind becomes clear. After this, you must breathe deeply to let go of anything stuck at your chest. You will come to a feeling of refreshment and a state of unity. In this state, if you proceed to *chinkon*, you will be lead to the "world of dawn" and begin feeling electric sensations at the fingers. Afterwards, this feeling will spread all over the body and you will feel as if someone is pouring energy over you. This is the power of spiritual strength (*miitsu*).

This method of *furitama* is effective in many aspects. First, utilizing the gap created between intense excitement and calmness, we "drill" inside of the heart. That is, we "open the soil of the heart" to make a hole there. Since various memories and thoughts have adhered to the inside of the heart layer after layer, we shake them up in order to make a hole there as preliminary work for the next practice of *chinkon*. In that next practice we explore the inside of the heart.

When we have strange body movements or postures during *furitama*, most cases indicate that we are straightening up our distorted body or changing the stagnated state of *ki* energy. This is the so-called "exercise of health building."

These days, people tend to lack physical exercise, so they can use this method for their health since intense body movement in *furitama* is effective for activating the body and psyche. However, people with asthma, heart disease, high blood pressure, or who have just recovered from sickness should avoid doing this common *furitama*.

There is also a special style of *furitama* for people who have been in physical recovery, even if they have been sick in bed for a long time. They should put their palms together in the bed and vibrate the palms very gently for a short time (one or two minutes). It will give a very light vibration to the whole body to loosen up the stiffness.

Another approach is to have a helper put the two feet of a sick person together. The helper grips the big toes and then swings them side to side for a short time.

This exercise stimulates the intestines. There are many patients who have rapidly recovered their health with this technique.

Conducting *furitama* over a period of one hundred days will yield the following benefits:

> Mental indolence will disappear and one will feel more vitality.
> Spiritual poison will be dispersed, so the body will become light.
> Chronic health problems will improve.
> Facial skin will become healthy and beautiful, and the skin color will lighten.
> Tired looking, loose skin will change into healthy looking skin.
> Bad posture will be corrected and geriatic posture will disappear.
> Eyes will become clear and strong in appearance.

Furitama is effective, then, not only for spiritual training but also for maintaining physical health.

The breathing method

In Shinto, as in *shinsendo*, yoga and *kiko* (*qigong*), breathing is important. The Shinto method, called "the method of *okinaga*" (long breathing) is simple and effective to practice.

First, you should exhale. The Japanese word for breathing is *kokyu* (呼吸: the two characters in *kokyu* mean exhale and inhale). Since ancient times it has been understood that you must first thoroughly exhale to effectively practice the breathing method.

Breathe in lightly through the nostrils and breathe out through the mouth. Do not breathe out quickly at once, but exhale gradually for a rather long time. Keep exhaling completely to the point that you feel you cannot exhale any longer. You may even bend your body a little bit forward. At this point you have to breathe in. Again, try to take as long as you can with a small amount of air inhaled gradually at each moment. Do not inhale all at once or in a hurry. Draw your abdomen back in order to push up the diaphragm. Inhale air to fill your whole chest. First conduct chest breathing, and stop inhaling when you have counted to the number 8. Then, bring the air from the chest down to the lower abdomen. Next, extend the abdomen out and tightly close the anus, again counting to the number 8. When you feel it is impossible to count further, exhale. Repeat this exercise about five times. This breathing method is called "the method of *shisoku*" (holding the breath). In yoga, it is called "pranayama."

Then carry out the next practice, *seisoku* (quiet breathing). With this method, begin from a complete exhale as in the above method. Then inhale slowly. This time, do not use chest breathing, but rather conduct abdominal breathing. It is important for you to take quiet and long breaths, and it is advisable that you count with the numbers *hi*, *fu*, *mi*, *yo*, *i*, *mu*, *na*, *ya*, *koto*, *tari*, *momo*, *chi*, *yorozu* (NOTE: this is the traditional Japanese way of counting numbers from 1 (*hi*) to 10 (*tari*), to 100, 1,000, and to 10,000). Count this way while quietly breathing in. After breathing in fully, concentrate firmly on *tanden* and close the anus tightly. Count up to number 10 and then exhale. Repeat this exercise about five times.

After you finish these two methods of breathing (*shisoku*—holding the breath, and *seisoku*—quiet breathing) continue the quiet and deep abdominal breathing. Soon your mind will become clearer and calmer. Gradually the state of breathing becomes closer to the state of non-breathing.

After this, we proceed to two other exercises, *godaiboin* (the five great vowels) and *goten gassho* (five tips of the fingers pressed to each other for a prayer to heaven). Later I shall discuss these two exercises in detail, but for now the crucial point is that one gets into *chinkon* with this quiet state of virtual non-breathing.

If the length of *chinkon* is about five minutes for beginners, that is fine. But it should be gradually increased. It is said that human beings can concentrate about two to three minutes, so one has to know how to bring back one's concentration when one loses it.

How to get rid of worldly thoughts

The conversation with the inner Kami (*naohinomitama*) takes the form of self-questions and self-answers. By asking questions to your own innermost heart/mind, without failure you will get answers from the inner Kami that express great wisdom.

However, worldly thoughts usually keep arising in the mind to interrupt inner concentration. It is therefore very difficult to have this conversation with inner-Kami. Sometimes thoughts can be knowledge and information you have acquired and stored in your heart and mind in layers that float off from the surface of each layer during *chinkon* practice. Sometimes you add modified ones, and you can even create images and stories that you yourself don't even remember. You can also create philosophical or logical contents that would surprise you. When you get these kinds of contents, great care is needed, because you might mistake them for the voice of Kami.

The human mind is, to begin with, constructed in a split or dichotomous way. One mind can criticize what the other mind is imagining. Or two minds can converse with each other within a self, whilst the third mind observes the conversation. The simplest means to get rid of these worldly thoughts is to ask them, "What do you have to do with me now?"

The worldly thoughts of a beginning practitioner don't amount to much, but magnificent words with apparent truths come to mind as you advance your spiritual training. Actually, these seemingly truthful words are also worldly thoughts in most cases. Casual ideas come to mind in the form of divine revelation or spiritual instruction, so it is difficult to deal with these. Therefore, when you think you have received divine revelation or spiritual instruction, you need to discern and evaluate it carefully. This discernment is called *saniwa* (the written characters mean "discernment of the divine"). It is very dangerous for a person to become arrogant without checking the authenticity of the message—you can play into the hands of low vibrating spirits.

Beginning with "one thought, one mind"

If you truly enter a deep state, then *chinkon* can also lead you into a realm exactly like the one known as "the realm of mindlessness and thoughtlessness." However, most people cannot reach this level even if they seek it. The capable instructor therefore tells the student, "First, concentrate your mind on one thought." In order to achieve this more easily, repeat the chanting of some appropriate words. In *koshinto* (ancient Shinto), the chant is called "the number song of heaven" and is recited over a long period of time. The words of the chant are: "*hi-fu-mi-yo-i-mu-na-ya-koto-tari-momo-chi-yorozu*": the numbers from *hi* to *tari* translate as one up to ten; *mono* is one hundred; *chi* is one thousand and *yorozu* is ten thousand. Another repetitious chant, the "five great vowels" (A O U E I) started being used during the Heian period (794–1185).

Sometimes simple repetition of a sound, such as that of a ticking clock or raindrops falling, is used in order to help with mental concentration. It is even possible to pick up a simple repetitive sound from surrounding noise and concentrate on it.

Another way of achieving mental concentration is simply by focusing on one thought. This practice means that a person focuses on only a pure and clean thought, which has nothing to do with mundane life thoughts. For example, a simple, grateful thought such as, "Kami, I truly thank you very much" would work for this purpose.

There are various ways one can develop mental concentration. When you successfully reach a concentrated mental state the realm "free from all ideas and thoughts" will be opened to you, even though it might be for only one or two seconds. This does not mean that you neither think nor feel in those moments. This realm is purely clean and bright, transparent everywhere, and filled with limitless wisdom. No matter how short the moment is, you can touch the eternally existing clean and bright world and feel that the entire universe exists within that brief period.

Various realms

If you continue *chinkon* practice you will experience many different realms. Each person has his or her own experience and, depending upon the person, the experiences are all different. We cannot necessarily say that a particular process is the right one. Some people might feel seized with a strange drowsiness while practicing *chinkon*. According to the orally transmitted instructions, if you fall asleep during the practice it may be just as well, although you shouldn't sleep until the end. You slip into a deep sleep and then wake up. At the point of contact between the drowsy state and the awakening state there is a subtle gap. If you slip into that gap, you enter a totally different world. This is also known as the "valley free from all ideas and thoughts."

Experiencing "light" is easy, even for beginners, during *chinkon*. One may experience the inside of the brain filled with dazzling light, or one may feel enveloped by a golden mist. But these are only preliminary states of consciousness. If you keep advancing from there by imagining a small sun or a round moon at the center of your forehead, eventually you will see a sun or moon of such brightness that you will be shocked. This does not appear as part of the realm of fantasy, but as the real experience it is. According to the hidden teaching handed down to the Yamakage family, people will see "mist, smoke, sun, wind, fire, fluorescence, crystal, and a moon." Sometimes a coal black experience may occur instead of light.

As for the state of heart and mind, it is possible to feel extremely exalted, or to have your eyes fill with tears. However, the better state of mind must be beyond any emotional manipulation and not at all confused and disturbed. In order to be able to be in this still state of mind, you need to keep a clear consciousness and not lose your rational faculty. There are some other states that you can experience during this time, such as the feeling of flying into a distant, high sky, or seeing something like a pure land of paradise, and so on. These experiences vary from person to person, and we cannot necessarily say which one is good or bad. As for proper discernment, you must be guided by an experienced and reputable instructor.

It is not good if people become attached to the experiences in the other worlds or seek this kind of experience too much. This annuls the whole purpose of the exercise, because it introduces a new attachment, which can arouse negative feelings of arrogance and pride. You should neither boast of yourself by talking about your own experience nor discuss whose experience is inferior or superior.

The secret knowledge of Yamakage Shinto

Yamakage Shinto includes other methods of practice. Traditionally, these belonged in the sphere of secret knowledge, imparted to only a few initiates. About thirty years ago, however, I decided to open three of these secrets to the public in order to try to teach as many people as possible. These are *goten gassho* (five tips of the fingers pressed to each other for a prayer to heaven), *godaiboin* (the five great vowels), and *dai-jinju* (the great divine incantation).

Goten gassho is the method for prayer in which the tips of all five fingers touch each other as they are held up over your forehead. You are making a magical finger posture with this method.

First, sit in either a relaxed or formal way. Stretch your arms to the sides and then bring them up and up, drawing a large arc. Then turn your palm toward heaven in order to feel the energy from above.

Goten gassho

Stretch the arms toward heaven as if you are embracing the sky. Do this last movement with the feeling of catching sky energy with both of your hands. Then gradually bring them down toward your forehead. When the fingers are approaching toward you, feel the energy that resembles something like electricity. When you bring these fingers down to the middle of the forehead (on the brow), you make the same magical posture as indicated before (see the figure for the *goten gassho* posture). You should visualize the whole universe contained inside the palms and with a great energy flowing into you through the middle of the forehead. In this way concentrate mentally for a while and put your thought on the great spirit of Kami (*daishirei*). Then bring your hands gradually down along the centerline of the body to *tanden*, a few inches down from the navel. (You may bring them down by drawing an arc in front of the body.) Visualize the energy of the universe as being stored in *tanden*.

The method of *godaiboin* involves chanting each vowel, "A-O-U-E-I" as long as you can in one breath. It is important to voice them out loud and from the bottom of your abdomen. You should chant this five times.

Daijinju (the great divine incantation) is the recitation of the sound "A-JI-MA-RI-KA-N," which I discussed in Chapter 5. In a formal way, during Shinto ceremonies in the Yamakage Shinto style, the sound *aji-marikan* is preceded by a longer recitation, which is the *daijinju* proper. You will find this recitation in Appendix 2.

Seeking the clean and bright heart/mind

What has been explained thus far is a summary of the systematic method of *chinkon* practice in Yamakage Shinto. By repeating this practice many times, you can bring the disorganized *shikon* (four souls) into focus and achieve serenity. You make *naohinomitama* (*ichirei*) shine more brightly. You gain the ability to communicate with the inner Kami. Although I have talked about various mystical experiences in this book, you should not think that a mystical experience is the only goal. It has its own meaning, but the goal for Shintoists is a "clean and bright heart/mind." Being overly concerned with logic and details or dressing up in the robe of mysticism will be greatly harmful.

At the Yamakage Shinto School, where people are instructed in the practice of *chinkon*, we exclaim the following words very loudly after completing the practice of *furitama*:

"Ana Appare" (the characters of *appare* mean "clear sky");
"Ana Tanoshi" ("happy" or "stretching arms");
"Ana Omoshiro" ("white face", meaning "pleasant");
"Ana Saake" ("clean and bright");
"Oke!"

These words are taken from the book of *Kogoshui*. With this exclamation, your heart and mind will become bright and clear and the body and mind will be cleansed. When people achieve this state of mind, they can get rid of any problematic, worldly thoughts and make the clean and bright mind expand.

What are the characteristics of persons experiencing the deep realm?

Among those who come to practice *chinkon*, I occasionally find some who come for the practice in order to seek mystical experiences or manifest psychic power. They become proud of themselves by saying, "I saw light!" or "I heard a voice!" However, these are merely illusions they created through the combined work of their unconscious desires and their knowledge.

Even if you are not this kind of person, you have to verify whether or not various experiences during *chinkon* are real or merely the continuation of your worldly thoughts. You have to know that we human beings are really very much in the realm of illusion. We cannot easily discern whether we are advancing to higher levels through our training or not.

As for the human being's unification with Kami gained through *chinkon* practice, it is certainly an individual, subjective experience. Therefore it is difficult to judge whether or not it is a deep or shallow experience, or true or false.

Through my experience, I can tell that those who have advanced spiritually and have the experience of the deep realm show clearly detectable and objective signs of their advancement. These signs are as follows:

1. This person radiates cleanness and purity from all over his or her body.
2. During meditation, this person's figure stands out in the dimly lit atmosphere.
3. During meditation, I can see this practitioner clearly radiate white light from the head to the shoulders.
4. The practitioner's view of life becomes very clear, and the person is not caught up by and swayed by outside events.
5. The person's emotional life becomes calm and tranquil, and the facial expression becomes warm and kind, so people feel calmness with this person's behavior and movement.

As for the "light" mentioned above in points 2 and 3, you will not be able to see that light if you have not trained spiritually enough to gain that spiritual sensibility. Nevertheless, that light is an objective fact.

You often hear people say, "that person appears to be shining," or "today that person is shining." Actually, this kind of expression is not necessarily an abstract, literary description. Even people with normal sensibility feel the subtle vibration or light that is released around a person. Religious scholars without any spiritual experience or religious men armed only with form might negate such expressions by saying that such a thing does not exist. But if you continue your spiritual training, most people will discover that such a thing is quite normal. Most *chinkon* practitioners, after practicing continuously for about fifty days, begin to see a whitish light radiating around the shoulder, mainly at night and dusk, and even during daytime. This light is clear and lucid and very subtle.

The path to service

The most important feature to judge whether or not a person is coming closer to the level of unification with Kami is whether or not the character is well-formed and fully developed.

If you do not have a well-formed character, then neither mystical experiences nor psychic and spiritual power has any meaning at all. It is true that mystical experiences are wonderful. Experiencing the invisible worlds and coming into touch with a part of the structure of these worlds enriches people's lives. Psychic and spiritual power is also effective in solving various problems and in helping other people. However, it is often the case that you put yourself in serious danger if you are only caught up in psychic and spiritual powers. Psychic and spiritual power is nothing more than a human faculty. It is the same kind of ability that musically talented or athletically talented people have when they excel with those gifts. As we all might know, talented athletes are not necessarily men or women of character. In the same way, psychic power is not necessarily consistent with traits of good character. On the contrary, if you become showy about your psychic power and develop arrogance, then it will distort one's character and drag a person into the influence of spirits of a very low rank.

When people reach the truly deep realm of unification with Kami, they will not attach importance to that experience or the power that flows from it as ends in themselves. They understand that both experience and power can be meaningful only in the context of the harmony of all existence. Furthermore, they realize their own ignorance and powerlessness, and they come to understand the greatness of Kami's work. Gratitude and affection toward all that is created by Kami then must spring from them. In other words, if harmony, gratitude, and service are not well understood and comprehended by them, then we cannot say that they have reached the state of true unification with Kami.

The human experience of the realm of unification with Kami is only the first stage of the journey. We need to move on to "the life of service." In Shinto, we follow after the example of the will and action of Kami in order to become like Kami. We also serve the work of the invisible Kami.

Service does not have to be elaborate or large-scale. It can be simple voluntary work or showing kindness to people around you. What is important is neither the outside appearance nor the effectiveness of that service. What counts is rather the practice of gratitude overflowing from your own heart, free from arrogance, and stemming from thoughts of altruism.

What is prayer?

This is a suitable time to address the question of prayer, or *norito*, in Shinto.

Reciting the ritual prayer or the great divine incantation (*daijinju*) during *chinkon* practice is about much more than mental concentration. Another important aspect of the ritual is purification (*harai*) through the spirit of the word (*kotodama*). At the bottom of this action is the need for sincere prayer toward Kami.

True prayer is neither calling "Kami, Kami" with a loud shouting voice nor chanting an incantation from the sacred books with eyes upturned and in front of a shrine or statue. However sincere this might appear, these types of prayer are not necessarily the most correct or effective ways. The right way of prayer is to pay respect to Kami as if your yearning feeling for Kami flows from the bottom of your soul. Soul is, in a sense, like a broadcast station. Our thoughts and feelings are always emitted as a spiritual thought wave. They are usually no more than a wild noise. However, if you pour abundant love and respect toward Kami into the soul, this love and respect will reach even to the end of the universe. This type of prayer is considered the right one. So, first of all, prayer must involve speaking toward your own interior and thinking with your whole heart/mind.

This mind-concentration is quite difficult for us to achieve. Some say that the limit of human mental concentration is about two minutes. It happens that worldly thoughts arise in your mind during the process of mental concentration, just as during *chinkon* practice.

There are several ways to practice mind-concentration. One is repeating words tens and hundreds of times by entrusting intense thought to the words. Or one can listen to one's voice of prayer intently and with mental concentration. Or you can imagine the Kami that you are praying to. For example, you could think that Kami appears as a shining sphere of white light and imagine this while praying.

As for *daijinju*, for example, the great divine incantation (*ajimarikan*) that I described before, when you chant it intently with a concentrated mind and pray as you listen to your own voice, a murmuring voice will soon flow into your ears and within your voiced prayer. Sometimes it can be a voice like a ringing bell. When you reach this level you will not feel your surroundings and you will be led into a realm of ecstasy. You will feel the prayer flowing like a wave within you.

However, all these methods are just devices. Prayer is actually your talk to your own inner Kami, so it has to be discharged with a quiet voice, even a murmur. For example, the prayer of *noro*, the priestesses of Okinawa, is done in such a quiet voice that even people right beside her cannot tell what kind of prayer she is offering to Kami.

During *chinkon* practice, you do not offer the "dedication of gratitude toward Kami" in a loud voice either. You have to talk to Kami in a murmur that comes from the innermost part of your heart. Also, when chanting the great divine incantation, *ajimarikan*, for your mental concentration, you do so in a soft voice. Then you will get good results. However, the spirit of the words, or *kotodama*, is of utmost importance in Shinto, so it is critical to have correct pronunciation for each sound.

Prayer as a dedication of gratitude toward Kami

Certainly there is a prayer through which people express their wish to Kami and wish that their prayers be answered. You fill your heart and mind with only the thought toward Kami and pray single-mindedly. Your prayer will reach to the spirit of Kami without failure. We can say that "prayer never fails if it goes through to Kami." Since ancient times it has been said that "egoistic prayer never goes through." It is true that any selfish desire without one taking responsibility will probably be ignored by the spirit of Kami. Another point to note is that the answered prayer does not necessarily manifest in the same way as you wanted it to. However, if you pray to Kami with your whole heart and mind, your prayer will never fail to go through to Kami.

Prayer with the whole heart and mind means that you surrender yourself and commit everything to the care of Kami. There is a saying that one should commit oneself "at the risk of one's life," but in reality it should not be so much of a burden. What is important is that you pray with abundant love and with the attitude of dedicating yourself to Kami. The prayer can be for healing an illness of a family member or for the passing of an entrance examination to a particular school or company. If you pray not from shallow egoistic desire but with total surrender of yourself, committing everything to Kami's care, the spirit of Kami will surely respond.

Sincere wishes are truly realized

There is another type of prayer. This involves your pledge to yourself and the demonstrations of the power of your own spirit-soul. In order to have this prayer answered, there should be complete belief and confidence that the wish will be answered. That is, the prayer has the status of a wishing prayer that is crystal-clear and already realized. To put it simply, you must think at the deep level of your heart, "this has already been realized and is definite," and believe it completely.

Human thoughts are, in a sense, extremely powerful. What you truly believe may be realized without failure. This may sound improbable, but it really is so. In cases where things are not going as you wish, you might not want what you think you want, or you might be held back by the unconscious belief that your wishes will never be fulfilled. If you are determined about something from the bottom of your heart and you can maintain determination for a long time, it will certainly be realized. This is the power of the human mind, and the power of the human spirit-soul.

In this way, wishes are definite and already realized. One should proceed with a concentrated mind and maintain it in the same way every day.

Prayer is not an act of speaking loudly with eyes upturned, but rather one of thinking quietly and intensely. This thinking and praying will eventually enter one's sub-consciousness.

What to do when you visit a shrine to pay respect to Kami?

Before entering the shrine, you must wash your hands and mouth at the special place for *temizu*, (ritual of washing hands). First wash your left hand and then the right hand by pouring water from a ladle. Then, holding water in the left hand, pour it into your mouth. This is a simple *misogi*, an act of purifying the body, heart, and mind in front of Kami.

Then you proceed toward the place of worship in front of the shrine building, bow two times there and clap your hands two times. Afterwards you bow deeply and offer words of gratitude. This is a basic way of worshipping at a shrine. Reciting prayers such as the words for purification (*misogi harai no kotoba*) or the congratulatory address to Kami is a slightly higher-level method of paying respect at a shrine. If you pray for your wish it is important to mention your whole name and address before your prayer. After the prayer, bow two times, clap two times, and conclude with a final bow.

If you apply to the administration of a shrine for formal worship, the shrine will let you practice *tamagushihoten*. The word *hoten* means "respectfully offer something to Kami."

Tamagushi is a branch of the *sakaki*, an evergreen tree native to Japan, with *shide* (paper cut in a special way) attached to it. This offering is placed on the table that is set in front of the shrine. When you receive the *tamagushi*, your left hand supports the leaf part and the right hand holds the branch stalk. Proceed to the front of the shrine, bow deeply, and then turn the *tamagushi* three-quarters clockwise. You should offer *tamagushi* in such a way that the root of the sacred sprig is facing toward the shrine. Then you bow two times, clap two times, and then bow again. Usually the *kannushi* (Shinto master) at the shrine is on hand to give additional instructions.

As I have pointed out, however, going to just any shrine to worship is not recommended. There is a particular spiritual line or relationship for each person. We should conduct these personal prayers or wishing prayers at the shrine of our choice, according to our own spiritual line. The choice of protective shrine is decided through this spiritual tie or association. If one goes to any shrine indiscriminately and prays there, it will not work. Also, a visitor might decide to pray at a shrine during a sightseeing trip merely because it happens to be a famous shrine. I do not recommend such devotions, because it is possible to draw into oneself strange, low-ranking spirits residing at that shrine. Devotional visits to a shrine must therefore have a clear purpose and not take place on a whim.

Shinto practitioners will nonetheless inevitably find themselves at shrines with which they have no personal connection. In such situations, they should offer heart-felt gratitude to the local Kami for protecting its own place or people.

Prayer is *chinkon*

Once you master the right way of praying, your inner *naohinomitama* shines, and Kami's light beams inside your heart and mind. Prayer is also a work of purification and *chinkon*. If you get into the state of pure prayer and hear a sound like the tinkle of a golden bell, your inner mind will be filled with waves of love, harmony, truth, and peace, which are the true nature of Kami. Then the darkness within the mind and heart disappears, as if the sun was breaking the night. Your heart and mind will be filled with joy and gratitude. Bathed with the love and goodness that is Kami's life penetrating through heaven and earth, you will understand how ignorant human beings are when they hate or quarrel against one another.

Therefore it is important to make time for prayer, even if you cannot sit down to practice *chinkon* at all. In the midst of life's daily routines, make for introspective moments, offering your thought whole-heartedly to Kami. Repeating this practice day after day is surer than any ascetic path to purify your spirit-soul and receive the grace of Kami.

Looking steadily into your inner mind is *chinkon*

Once again, *chinkon* is the stilling of the mind at *tanden* and the rebalancing of the four souls. This will make *naohinomitama*, the *wake-mitama* of Kami within you shine. With the practice of *chinkon*, and through conversation with the inner Kami, you purify and cultivate your spirit-soul. You do this by receiving Kami's light and learning the values of gratitude and harmony.

Thus true *chinkon* practice takes place in your heart and mind. You should neither become obsessed with external formality, nor boast of your spiritual and psychic power or experience. It is a mistake either to aim at gaining supernatural power or to compare your own abilities with those of others. You must not become trapped in arrogant pride, nor become a slave to the process of spiritual training, nor speak noisily about its benefits. *Chinkon* should lead us to a state of spiritual calm, where selfish ambitions and desires give way to the realization of the true self, the Kami within each one of us.

Afterword

Shinto is not a faith tradition that can be propagated or imposed. Each human community, every human culture, has its own version of Shinto, which is based on accumulated experience, historical memory, and, perhaps most crucially, the local environment. Shinto recognizes and celebrates human diversity, just as it recognizes and celebrates the diversity of nature. For beneath that diversity there is an underlying unity—the union of humanity, earth, and heaven.

In the 1970s I accepted a few pupils from abroad to study Shinto with me. One of them was Paul de Leeuw, coeditor of this book. From the beginning I had insisted that he should discover his own Shinto. My aim in making this book accessible to the Western world is similar. I would like Westerners to discover their own version of Shinto, both within themselves and in their surroundings. By doing so, they will assist in the preservation and continuity of all life.

This book is an English translation and rendition of my book *Shinto no Shinpi*: *Essence of Shinto*, published in 2000 by Shunjusha in Tokyo, a publisher that specializes in works of a philosophical and spiritual nature. The original Japanese was first rendered into English by Mrs.

Mineko Shinmura Gillespie and Mr. Gerald L. Gillespie of the United States, and revised by Drs. Paul de Leeuw, of the Japanese Dutch Shinzen Foundation in Amsterdam, together with Mr. Yoshitsugu Komuro from Japan. The editor of the English edition is Dr. Aidan Rankin, of London, and Kodansha International of Tokyo has introduced the book to the world by publishing it. I am very grateful to all the individuals and organizations that have contributed to the completion of this book.

Finally, I would like to say a few words about Paul de Leeuw. In 1979, he came to Japan to practice Shinto. After several years I granted him a license to perform Shinto ceremonies and he became the first *kannushi*, or Shinto master, in Europe. Several Japanese companies with a European base, amongst them Takenaka, Kikkoman, Panasonic, and Fujifilm, have commissioned him to perform ceremonies to bestow good fortune on their premises during their construction and use, and protect those who build and work in them. In 2005 he performed the new year Shinto ceremony at the Hotel Okura, Amsterdam, an event that attracted many Dutch people, as well as Japanese residents in Holland and even from all over Europe. His pioneering work has convinced me of the rightness of my original idea that Shinto cannot be propagated, but should be rediscovered in each country as its spiritual heart.

Motohisa Yamakage

Notes

1. Every child reaching the ages of three, five, and seven is taken to the shrine for a ritual ceremony.

2. "*Bun*" means "to impart, share, or separate." Therefore "*bunrei*" is the spirit separating from or emerging out of the spirit of Kami of its parent(s). Further, the spirit of Kami imparts a spirit as a child-spirit to the lower world. This child-spirit will then become a parent spirit for the next child spirit to be sent to a place such as a small-scale shrine.

3. The late Professor Jean Herbert of Geneva University in Switzerland made a distinction between two types of divided spirit:

   1) A physical or geographical division in which shrine Y is a branch of shrine X; in these cases, the spirit of shrine Y is called the divided spirit of shrine X;

   2) Man as a divided soul in the sense the he is one facet of the universal organic body called *daigenrei* (the original Kami). He is therefore part of the universal spirit, but also has a distinctive identity.

   Because of this distinction we, as Shintoists, discovered that it was very difficult for Professor Herbert to understand the true meaning of "divided spirit." Within his terms of reference the divided spirit could not have the same qualities as the original spirit and, what is more, the original spirit cannot be divided at all. His understanding, influenced by Western binary logic, made it more difficult for him to experience the true relation of the divided spirit and the original spirit. In explaining that relationship, we drew a parallel with the relationship between seeds and trees. Each seed contains the potential to grow into a tree, and each tree has grown to maturity from a seed.

But there is always a continuity between the two forms: there is no sudden transformation from a seed into a tree, only an organic growth from one into another. This can be likened to the relationship between the divided spirit and the original spirit.

Professor Herbert still insisted upon the difference between the two forms, comparing the distribution of the seeds of the tree with the relationship between parents and children. He was still convinced that man as a divided soul is distinct from the original soul.

Citing Indian philosophy, he spoke of the universal spirit and the personal soul, Brahman and Atman. He explained that in Indian philosophy the personal souls (or inner deities) do not have the same capacity for growth as is attributed to them by Shinto. That is why the divided spirit cannot have the same qualities as the universal or original spirit. He preferred to see man as "another self of deity," and the individual self as the "individual energy derived from the universal self." Man is a micro cosmos, having the same capacity for growing as the macro cosmos (e.g. the milky way). However, both are finally destined to perish. For the same reason he doubted that a human being could have the ability to enshrine in shrine Y the Kami of shrine X.

Finally we concluded that it is very difficult to reconcile the two different mindsets. In the Western frame of reference, religious belief is mainly thought to be based upon the idea of god as a trinity, while Shinto experiences the continuity of the divided spirit and the original spirit. This continuity is elaborated in the philosophy of *ichirei shikon*: one spirit, four souls.

4. Gaia was the goddess of earth in Greek mythology. Lovelock's Gaia theory postulated that earth's life support systems (including the oceans, air, and the elements) are somehow internally controlled, and regulate the radiation balance of earth to keep it habitable.

5. *Yorishiro is* a spiritual antenna that receives the spirit of Kami and bestows its presence to this world.

6. *Harai* means literally: dusting off, driving out evil spirits or shaking off contaminating influences.

7. The Character "shin" means "Kami" and "rei" means "spirit," hence *shinrei* = "spirit of Kami" and *Shinto* = way of Kami.

8. Happiness and honesty as part of the expression *jo-mei-sei-choku* will be explained in Chapter 3.

9. *Keihitsu*: "breathing out with the sound 'oh!' as an invocation for the spirit of Kami."

10. See Chapter 7 about the various worlds of spirits of Kami.

11. For more on the concept of clean and bright see Chapter 4 about *misogi*.

12. See Appendix 1 for the Yamakage Shinto Practice.

13. See Chapter 6 for a detailed description of the four different soul levels.

14. The Japanese writer Yasushi Inoue (1907–92) wrote a short story "Passage to Fudaraku" about the practice in the 16th century of Buddhist monks setting sail from the south Kumano coast with the pure land, known as Fudaraku, as their destination. The story can be found in Lou-lan and Other Stories by Yasushi Inoue, translated by James T. Araki. (Kodansha International 1987.)

15. "Excite" is "*furuiokosu*" in Japanese.

16. *ama* = heaven; *uzu-uzushi* = whirling, volute, spiral; *ya* = eight, in all directions, or the whole universe; *tsunagi* = link, connect, tie; *ame* = heaven; *mi-oya* = parent; *o-Kami* = great Kami; *tsu* and *no* = of.

Appendix I

The many names of Kami

From ancient times, the Japanese have possessed a wide spiritual vocabulary, with a rich repository of words to express the sacred dimension. The spirit-soul (*reikon*), for instance, is referred to as follows:

mi

This is the most sacred name, expressing the source and essence of life.

The fountainhead Kami of the universe who is the first in the divine lineage is called *Amenominakanushi no kami*. This is usually interpreted as *ame* for an honorary title, *mi* as an honorific word, *nakanushi* as the adjective, and Kami as the main word. But this interpretation is not appropriate. We should interpret this *mi* as the main word and all others as modifiers.

hi or *bi*

The written characters for this name convey the meaning of "fire," "sun," "spirit," and some others. Originally this meant "something essential for sustaining and energizing life." As I explained earlier, *musubi* means the creation and development (*seisei kaiku*) of life (*hi* means the same as *bi*). The two Kami who follow after *Amenominakanushi no kami* are called *Takamimusubi* and *Kamimusubi*.

The character used to write the names of each of these two Kami is again different depending on the text, so it often confuses people. But in either case, the real meaning is this: the character for *Taka* means "manifestation" and the character for *Kamu* means "subtle, deep, hidden, and invisible."

Therefore, each represents the yin and yang, the complimentary principles associated with Taoist philosophy but also recognized in Shinto. When *Taka* (yang) and *Kamu* (yin) unite (*musu* + *bi* (*hi*) = unite) they form the essential core that is *mi*. This is very much like the situation of the Big Bang in which an original source point separates into two to create all things. These two "Kami of *musuhi*" have created all life and phenomenon.

It is worth noting here that this *hi* coalesces with *to-(domaru)*—meaning "come to completion"—into a form that is the so-called *hi-to*, meaning "human being." Therefore human beings are considered to have been endowed with the essential spirit of Kami.

chi

This is the spirit-soul (*reikon*) of the nature-Kami, which is highly sacred and which is equal to *mi* and *hi*. This can be seen in *Kukunuchi no kami* (Kami of Tree) and *Kagutsuchi no kami* (Kami of Fire).

tama

This is the spirit-soul dwelling inside human beings or animals.

mono

This is the name or title for anything that resembles spirit-soul in its effects or character. It is similar to a spirit-soul, but not identical to the pure spirit-soul. For instance, *mononoke* is the bad vibration that is released from a wicked thought or spirit.

Kami

This is the name for the spirit-soul that is hidden, unseen, and has a sacred as well as awe-inspiring effect. This name is a rather recent one compared to other ancient ones.

mikoto

This word from ancient times is equivalent to our present term, "Kami." Ancient people used this word for "Kami." This word is built up from two different characters: "life" and "reverence or honor." However, these characters do not reveal the real meaning of *mikoto*. It should be interpreted by understanding that *koto* means both "words and language," as well as "worldly events." *Mikoto* is someone who receives words or messages about events (or **koto**) from the Divine, or **mi**. The title *mikoto* should be used, therefore, for those Kami who have the status and character of a human being and who act in this world. The character for Kami (神) represents the "lightning flash coming down from heaven (sky)," so Kami exactly should only refer to heavenly-Kami (or *tenjin*). Therefore there is some aberration in this meaning if we use the title Kami for a human being acting in this world. All this said, we can now say that the title *mikoto* is a more ancient one than the title Kami.

nushi

This is used for the principal, major spirit-soul (*reikon*), which has much of the sacred power of *mi*, *hi*, and *chi*.

The hierarchy of Kami

Japanese spirituality has always recognized that Kami come in different forms, shapes, and sizes, and have different roles and functions. The spiritual dimension, the world of Kami, permeates all life forms, including humans, animals, and plants. All forms of life are interconnected and interdependent. The same is true of Kami.

Since ancient times, Shinto has drawn a distinction between *amatsukami* (heavenly Kami) and *kunitsukami* (earthly Kami). The assumption and interpretation here is that even in the Kami world there are different roles for *kamigami* (plural for Kami). One group of *kamigami* is in the higher-level world called *Takamano-hara* and the other remains closer to this material world and is active here.

In the great purification words (*oharai no kotoba*) it is said:
"when we chant the 'heavenly prayer words' (*amatsu norito*), *amatsukami* will listen to this prayer after pushing the Heavenly Rock Door open, cutting through the eight-fold thick cloud in the heaven; *kunitsukami* will listen to this prayer after climbing up to the ridge of high and low mountains and clearing the mist surrounding the mountains."

During the medieval era, following influence from Buddhism, Shinto developed the concept of the "realistic (actual) one" (*jissha*) and the "provisional, assumed one" (*gonsha*) in Kami. And—again due to the dominance of Buddhism at that era—the sacred one is *Nyorai* (Buddha) and the rest of them are *gonsha*, meaning "temporally manifested ones." *Jissha* "realistic /actual one" in the Shinto tradition actually means animal spirits in most cases. But from the perspective of the "unified Shinto/Buddhism" that emerged in these times, Japanese *kamigami* are considered to be *gongen* (temporal manifestations). For at that time, a synthesis of Shinto and Buddhism emerged, which developed a distinctive spiritual approach. Within that framework, however, the indigenous Japanese *kamigami* were regarded as inferior to their Buddhist counterparts, since Buddhist values were dominant in Japan at that time.

The Japanese also saw images of Kami in common places and in tools used for everyday life, and felt the presence of Kami in animals and plants. For example, there were Kami "families" of the fox and badger. These two species are therefore regarded as sacred by many Shinto practitioners. Also, the spirits of the rice plant or silk worms were important for daily living—these were also Kami in the Japanese belief. Surrounding a village, there was *Saenokami* who kept the village from the intrusion of evil. For the kitchen cooking stove, there was a Kami that kept the house safe. The Japanese also believed that spirits also dwelled in the well-worn tools that were used daily.

Japanese spirituality therefore recognizes the presence of Kami at levels of existence and consciousness, assuming an infinite variety of roles and functions. There is in the world of Kami a great chain of being, just as there is in the material world that humans inhabit.

Polytheism and monotheism

It is said that Shinto is polytheistic and therefore that the Japanese are polytheists. This is because there are many forms and levels of Kami, rather than a single divine power. The many spirits of Kami, however, do not have the independence characteristic of some polytheistic systems. Instead, each one has its own function as part of a hierarchy or chain of being.

At the source of this hierarchy, there is one Kami, supreme and the origin of all, with the name *Amenominakanushi no okami*. The next two Kami came out of the one as functions unfolding the yin and yang of *Amenominakanushi no okami*. They are called *Takamimusubi no okami* and *Kamimusubi no okami*.

We consider these three Kami as "three creator-Kami" and in Yamakage Shinto they are called the Kami of the threefold whirl, or *Amatsu uzu-uzushiyatsunagi no ameno mi-oya no o-kami*,[16] or *daigenrei* (the great original spirit). They are the Kami from which all natural phenomena arise. Since they are the true reality, we also call them *jisshin* (real Kami).

There are Kami who reflect and express the work of this *jisshin* (*daigenrei*) and who "generate, grow, transform, and cultivate everything and all phenomenon." These Kami are called *Narimasukami* (the written character for *narimasu* literally means "to transform and become," that is, "to be created"). The most important *Narimasukami* are the last two of the first five Kami (The first three of this five Kami are creators or *jisshin*). Other *Narimasukami* are the seven generations of earthly Kami (*chishin nanadai*).

The first five Kami, which include *jisshin*, the three creators, are called "five generations of heavenly Kami" (*tenshin godai*). For an overview of these Kami, see the systematic table of *ichirei shikon* in Chapter 6. Although the original Kami of the threefold whirl might be said to resemble a divine trinity, they are better interpreted by the philosophy of one spirit, four souls. *Amenominakanushi no okami* is the one spirit, while *Takamimusubi no okami* (as a combination of *kushimitama* and *aramitama*) and *Kamimusubi no okami* (as a combination of *sachimitama* and *nigimitama*) represent the four souls.

To the *Narimasukami* also belong all Kami of the great nature, such as the Kami of the mountain (*Oyamazumi no kami* and *Oyamagui no kami*) and the Kami of the ocean (*Owatatsumi no kami*). All of these *Narimasukami* are *bunshin* of real Kami (*jisshin*). This *bunshin* is the *yorishiro* (a spiritual antenna) where *daigenrei* (*jisshin*) can come down, in order to radiate its presence in this world.

Bunshin literally means "separated from or a part of Kami." It came out of *jisshin*, the real Kami (the great original spirit or *daigenrei*) like a child of Kami. In this way there is a line of spiritual inheritance by which *jisshin* manifests itself to this world through *bunshin* to carry out divine projects.

The Kami of wood, fire, earth, metal, and water are also *Narimasukami*, but they are not personified. Therefore they are called *shinki* (energetic essence of Kami) while other *Narimasukami* are called *shinrei* (spirit of Kami). We may also assume that human beings, as well as all other species and natural phenomena, are *Narimasukami* in the broadest sense, since they are created by real Kami and are also its reflection and manifestation.

To summarize, we can say that Shinto is at once polytheistic *and* monotheistic. It is the Shinto mystery as well as Shinto's inclusiveness that it accepts many (poly) and accepts one (mono).

It should be noted that in Shinto, generally speaking, *Amaterasu omikami* is looked upon as the "principal Kami." *Amaterasu omikami* is the sun-Kami and connected with the legendary founder of the imperial family, but there are lots of complicated circumstances surrounding this. Recent academic theory supports the notion that the peoples coming into Japan from the northern route took *Ameno-minakanushi no okami* as their supreme Kami, while those from the southern route took *Amaterasu omikami* as their supreme Kami. The mythologies of the *Kojiki* and *Nihonshoki* are a compromise between, or fusion of these two different cultures. This recent academic idea is probably true, but we should understand that this is not opposed to the older understanding, but rather integrated with it.

The sun is the source of all life and the greatest and most visible reflection of the creator Kami, the source. Also, the emperor's family who unified ancient Japan worshipped and revered *Amaterasu omikami*, so it is natural that this Kami became a principal Kami in Japan.

However, instead of *Amaterasu omikami* as Kami for the imperial founder there was originally a shamanistic queen, named *Ohirume no muchi*. She revered both the sun-Kami *Amaterasu omikami* and *Takamimusubi no okami*. In the course of time, the high priestess *Ohirume no muchi* and the sun-Kami (*Amaterasu omikami*) whom she revered gradually united to become one.

After *Okuninushi no mikoto* of Izumo yielded the chief position of the nation to the imperial founder, he vowed: "I shall yield this nation to *Amaterasu* and I shall become the chief of the other world." This is why *Amaterasu omikami* for the imperial founder became the chief Kami in Japan. Therefore, we treat *Amaterasu omikami* as the chief Kami at the Shinto ceremony and the ritual services in modern Japan. But we have to keep in mind that *Okuninushi no mikoto* actually controls every spiritual phenomenon.

Appendix II

Practice of *chinkon* at Yamakage Shinto training center

Although Shinto practice should be instructed by a qualified Shinto master, the reader may get an idea of it from the following outline:

1. *Misogi*, purification with water
2. Sit still for a while to achieve calm
3. Bow twice and clap the hands twice, and bow once again
4. Recite *misogi harai no kotoba* (words for purification)
5. Recite *oharai no kotoba* (words for great purification)
6. *Daijinju* and *ajimarikan*
7. *Furutama* (or *furitama*)
8. Breathing exercise
9. *Godai boin* (the five vowels A O U E I)
10. *Goten gassho*
11. Practice of *chinkon*
12. Breathing exercise
13. *Daijinju* and *ajimarikan*
14. *Goten gassho*
15. Bow twice and clap the hands twice, and bow once again
16. Sit still for a while

For a beginner it is absolutely crucial to be instructed by a qualified Shinto master, in order to get the best advice about sitting posture and breathing techniques.

There are also many details that can be handed down only in an oral way, since they belong to the so-called "secret tradition" of Yamakage Shinto, which means that they can be taught only to people who have proven worthy of receiving it.

Here I will provide the reader with some basic information. First I will give the text of the purification words, *misogi harai no kotoba* and *oharai no kotoba*, together with an English translation. This will be followed by some other texts to be used as a companion during *chinkon* practice.

Misogi harai no kotoba

JAPANESE

Kakemaku mo ayani kashikoki kamu Izanagi no okami

Tsukushi no himuka no tachihana no odo no awagi hara ni

Misogi haraishi tamau tokini aremaseru haraedo no okami tachi

Moromoro no magagoto tsumi toga kegare wo harai tamae kiyome tamae to mousu koto no yoshi wo

Amatsukami kunitsu kami yaoyorozu no kami tachi tomoni kikoshimese to mousu.

Tou kami emi tame harai tamae kiyome tamae.

TRANSLATION

By graciously pronouncing the name of *Izanagi no okami*, who purified himself by ablution in the calm sea in the morning sun, and the names of all the purification-Kami who came into existence during this purification, I express my humble wish to be purified myself from all disasters, mishaps, transgressions, faults, and defilements.

I ask all purification-Kami to forward my request of purification to *amatsukami* (heavenly Kami), *kunitsukami* (earthly Kami) and *yaoyorozu no kami* (the myriad other Kami). Most reverently I entreat all Kami to have my wish fulfilled.

Oharai no kotoba

JAPANESE

TAKAMA NO HARA NI KAMI ZUMARI MASU SUMERAGA MUTSU
KAMUROGI KAMUROMI NO MIKOTO MOCHITE.

Yaoyorozu no kamitachi wo kamutsudoe ni tsudoe tamai kamu hakarai ni hakari
tamaite agasumemima no mikoto wa toyo ashihara no mizuho no kuni wo
yasukuni to taira keku shiroshimese to koto yosashi matsuriki.

Kaku yosashi matsurishi kunuchi ni araburu kamu tachi wo ba kamu towashi ni
towashi tamai.

Kamu harai ni harai tamaite kototo ishi iwane kine tachi kusa no kakiha wo
mo koto yamete ame no iwakura hanachi ame no yaegumo wo izuno chiwaki ni
chiwakite amakudashi yosashi matsuriki.

Kaku yosashi matsurishi yomo no kuni nakata oyamato hitakami no kuni wo
yasukuni to sadame matsurite.

Shitatsu iwane ni miyahashira futoshiki tate takamano hara ni chigitaka shirite
sumemima no mikoto no mizuno miaraka tsukae matsurite.

Ame no mikage hi no mikage to kakuri mashite yasukuni to taira keku
shiroshimesam.

Kunuchi ni nari idem ame no masu hitora ga ayamachi okashikem kusugusa no
tsumi goto wa amatsu tsumi kunitsutsumi kokodakuno tsumi idem.

Kaku ideba amatsu miyagoto mochite amatsu kanagi wo moto uchi kiri sue uchi
tachite chikura no okikura ni okitara washite.

Amatsu sugaso wo moto karitachi sue kari kirite yahari ni tori sakite *amatsu
norito no futonorito* goto wo nore.

KAKU NORABA AMATSUKAMI WO AME NO IWATO WO OSHI HIRAKITE.

Ame no yaegumo wo izuno chiwaki ni chiwakite kikoshimesam.

Kunitsukami wa takayama no sue hikiyama no sue ni nobori mashite takayama no ihori hikiyama no ihori wo kakiwakite kikoshimesam.

Kaku kikoshimeshite wa tsumi to iu tsumi wa araji to shinado no kaze no ame no yaegumo wo ibuki hanatsu goto no kotoku.

Ashita no mikiri yube no mikiri wo asakaze yukaze no fuki harau goto no kotoku.

Otsube ni ori ofune wo hetoki hanachi tomo toki hanachite ounabara ni oshi hanatsu goto no kotoku.

Ochi kata no shigeki ga moto wo yakigama no togama mochite uchi harau goto no kotoku.

Nokoru tsumi wa araji to harai tamae kiyome tamau koto wo takayama no sue hikiyama no sue yori sakunadari ni ochi takitsu hayakawa no seni masu Seoritsu Hime to iu kami ounabara ni mochi idenam.

Kaku mochi ideinaba arashio no shio no yaoji no yashiojino shio no yaoai ni masu Haya Akitsu Hime to iu kami mochi kaka nomitem.

Kaku kaka nomitewa ibukido ni masu Ibukido Nushi to iu kami neno kuni sokono kuni ni ibuki hanachitem.

Kaku ibuki hanachitewa neno kuni sokono kuni ni masu Hayasasurai Hime to iu kami mochi sasurai ushinaitem.

Kaku sasurai ushinaitewa kyo yori hajimete tsumi to iu tsumi wa araji to harai tamae kiyome tamau koto wo.

Amatsukami kunitsukami yaoyorozu no kami tachi tomo ni ama no yahirade wo uchi agete kikoshimese to mousu.

TRANSLATION

Once there was in the high plain of heavens a couple of ancestral Kami, male and female, who ordered all Kami to assemble in a great meeting.

After everybody was consulted and all and everything was thoroughly discussed, they spoke the following words:

"Our sovereign grandchild will be entrusted the rule over the fertile earth in order to keep peace."

Overlooking the country that was entrusted to him, the great grandchild asked the unruly Kami of earth why they were so rebellious. Whenever he could not pacify them, he drove them out. So he conquered any resistance that was concealed behind rocks, under the roots of trees or in the reeds, until everything was calm.

Then he left his rock-seat in heaven. With his mighty power he pushed aside the many layers of thick clouds and descended from the heavens to the earth.

After his descent he ruled over the land of Yamato in such a way that it became the most radiant and most peaceful country on the earth.

Setting up pillars firmly in the rocks underground he built a beautiful palace and its roof rose high towards the high heavenly plain. Concealed within this palace that mirrors heaven and the sun, he reigned over the land that became a peaceful country.

Since then many people were born, who inevitably committed a lot of mistakes and transgressions, heavenly sins (*amatsu tsumi*) and earthly sins (*kunitsu tsumi*).

In order to purify the materialized bad vibrations resulting from these sins it is necessary to perform a duly prescribed ritual.

Firstly, cut the root and the top of the heavenly tree and make sticks of it. Assemble them to make a stand.

Next, cut off the bottom and top of the heavenly sedge reeds, and tear them into many strips.

Finally, recite the heavenly words, the solemn ritual words (*amatsu norito no futonorito*).

As soon as these solemn words are properly pronounced, the heavenly Kami will push the heavenly rock-door open and push aside the many layers of thick clouds, in order to hear and acknowledge the words of the ritual.

The earthly Kami will climb the mountains, the high and the low ones, and clear away the mist around the top, in order to hear and acknowledge the words of the ritual. As soon as the solemn words have been heard and acknowledged by the Kami of heaven and earth, the whole country will be purified from every kind of sin. It will be as if the Kami of the wind has blown away the thick clouds. It will be as if the morning fog and the evening fog are dispersed by a blast. It will be as if a big ship—after its ropes at the prow and the stern are cut—is pushed out from the harbor into the ocean. It will be as if a tree with lustrous leaves is cut at its base with a tempered sickle, a sharp sickle, and tumbles down from the hill. Likewise all sins and faults will fall down from mountains high and low, and will be taken away by the Kami *Seoritsu hime*, who dwells at waterfalls and rapids. She takes them away to the sea. There in the sea, they will be swallowed by the Kami *Hayaakitsu hime*, who dwells in the wild brine, the myriad currents of brine, in the myriad meeting places of the brine of many briny currents. After they are swallowed all the impurities are blown away by the Kami *Ibukidonushi*, who lives in *Ibukido*, until they reach the nether world. There lives the Kami *Hayasasura hime*, who will wander off with them and surely lose them finally.

Since they are finally lost by *Hayasasura hime no kami*, each and every sin has gone from now on. Likewise we pray in this solemn ritual to the heavenly Kami, the earthly Kami and the myriad other Kami that they hear us and grant our wish for purification.

Daijinju and *ajimarikan*

JAPANESE

Shishin shisei ishin hoto jintsu jizai shinriki shinmyo kamno sokutsu nyoi zuigan kettei joju

Mujo reiho Shinto kaji daigen genki genmyo shishin shiseino myotai

Ajimarikan

TRANSLATION

Establishing true communication with Kami

Whenever we address Kami with heart and soul and with a sincere mind, we establish an open way to connect with Kami. With his mysteriously deep power the Kami will reply immediately. Whenever we truly want something, it will be realized as soon as we have expressed the wish. As long as we live with a pure mind, Kami will protect us with his power and energy. This establishes a connection with the original source of energy, the hidden origin of the universe or *daigenrei*, who will come down to us and will radiate within us with a sincere mind.

Ajimarikan cannot be translated.

Yamakage Shinto acknowledges that it is very hard to keep concentration during *chinkon* practice. To solve this problem we recommend to alternate silent practice with another practice using the voice. The practice of making the sound *ajimarikan* may lead you to deep concentration. This concentration is even deepened if combined with a special gesture of the hands. However, this gesture belongs to a secret tradition that can only be transmitted directly from teacher to practitioner. The origin and exact meaning of *ajimarikan* are unknown. In ancient times *koshinto* instructed the new emperor to recite this chant during the *daijosai*, the ritual of enthronement. The chant is endowed with a particular, mysterious rhythm and resonance. After a while, one can hear a whirling vibration, sometimes

THE ESSENCE OF SHINTO

accompanied by the sound of tinkling silver bells. If you listen attentively to this sound, and surrender to its whirling vibration, you may plunge into another level of consciousness that opens up the way to *chinkon*.

Another variation of *chinkon* practice is a chant called the "counting of heavenly numbers" (*amano kazoeuta*).

Ama no kazoeuta

JAPANESE
Hito Futa Mitsu Yotsu
Itsu Mutsu Nana Yatsu
Kokono Tari Momo Chi Yorozu

Hito Futa Mitsu Yotsu Itsu Mutsu
Nana Yatsu Kokono Tari Momo Chi Yorozu

Hito Futa Mitsu Yotsu Itsu Mutsu Nana Yatsu Kokono Tari Momo Chi Yorozu

TRANSLATION
The translation is rather simple:
1 2 3 4 5 6 7 8 9 10 100 1000 10000

The aim of this practice is to obtain a quiet way of breathing. At the beginning one is able to count from 1 to 10 at every exhalation, but gradually one can make a jump from 1–100, or even from 1–1000 counts at every exhalation, until one feels the exhalation continues beyond the edge of the horizon—which is the deeper meaning of *yorozu*.

Dedication of gratitude toward Kami

Perhaps the practice of this prayer is the most vital gift of *koshinto* to our modern times. The words are not written down, but should come from the bottom of your heart. One of the most secretly kept rituals in *koshinto* is the mirror exercise. You sit in front of the mirror and start to look calm and quietly at your mirror image. After a while you make a bow and say in your mother tongue: "thank you very much." Someday you will realize that your mirror image reflects the inner Kami. "I am truly who I am." This realization can be stimulated by the practice of saying thanks to Kami, in a way as taught by the Yamakage Shinto *chinkon* practice.

Shinto practice aims at the fusing of two mirrors: the "Kami mirror" and "my mirror." Once that is accomplished, you will receive more and more of the cosmic energy. But what are you going to do with that energy? It should be used to help people around you, as if you have become a mirror to shine like the sun, reflecting the sunshine. After my first student from outside Japan, Paul de Leeuw from The Netherlands, had finished the one hundred days *chinkon* practice in my Yamakage Shinto Center, I strongly encouraged him to write a book about his experience. At the time of publication, I had suggested him to give it the title "I am a Mirror" (*Ware wa kagami nari*). The book is a sincere dedication of gratitude toward Kami.

The spiritual practice of Yamakage Shinto includes a series of hand postures (*mudra*), symbolizing spiritual development as it should be. This practice can be transmitted only directly from teacher to practitioner. Becoming the cosmic mirror itself is truly a dynamic drama, performed to manifest the process of growth of the inner cosmos, which has neither a beginning nor an end.

Additional Terms

Amatsukami	天津神	Heavenly Kami.
bunrei	分霊	Child-Spirit; everything in existence is generated by and transformed from the Ultimate Origin of Life; every (human) being has a full-fledged potential to become Kami; all forms of life are a Child-Spirit of original Kami.
chigi	千木	Part of Shinto architecture.
chinkon	鎮魂	*Koshinto* meditation to become aware of the existence of the Other World.
goshintai	ご神体	Body of Kami; material object representing the Spirit of Kami.
guji	宮司	Most senior master of a Shinto Shrine.
hakuhei	白幣	"Spiritual antenna," or *yorishiro*, made of paper.
harai	祓い	Purification (see Chapter 5).
himorogi	神籬	The spiritual antenna by which the Spirit of Kami can descend and manifest its presence. See *Yorishiro*.
hitogata	人型	Paper cut in the form of a human body.
ichirei shikon	一霊四魂	The principle of one spirit, four souls. The one

spirit, or core soul, is called *naohinomitama*; the four souls are respectively: *kushimitama*, *sachimitama*, *nigimitama* and *aramitama* (see Chapter 6).

iwakura	岩坐	Rock seat, functioning as *yorishiro*.
jinja	神社	Shinto shrine, a dwelling place for Kami.
joensai	浄焔祭	Fire ceremony practiced in Yamakage Shinto for purification.
kagami	鏡	Mirror.
kagura	神楽	Traditional Japanese music.
kamidana	神棚	Kami-shelf or household shrine.
kamigami	神々	Plural form of Kami.
kamihitogata	紙人型	Paper object, cut in the form of a human being.
kamizane	神核	"Kami's core." acting as a substitute or *katashiro* for Kami.
kannabi	神奈備	Special place where the Spirit of Kami descends to make its presence felt.
kannusa	神幣	Purification tool.
kannushi	神主	Male or female person functioning at a Shinto shrine; Shinto master.
katsuogi	鰹木	Typical part of Shinto architecture.
kegare	汚れ	Impurity, pollution, the material traces of bad vibrations, which must be cleaned by *harai* or *misogi*.

Kojiki	古事記	Ancient Chronicles of Japan, 712 (English translation by Donald Philippi).
koshinto	古神道	The oldest line of Shinto branches, a tradition that values the systematic methods of exercise and training.
kotodama	言霊	Spirit of the words.
kunitsukami	国津神	Earthly Kami.
magutsubi	禍津毘	Curved spirit, seen as the origin of evil deeds, misfortune, and disaster.
Man'yoshu	万葉集	Collection of short poems from early Japan.
misogi	禊ぎ	Self-purification with water.
mononoke	物の怪	Bad vibrations caused by vengeful ghosts.
musubi	ムスビ (結び, 産霊)	The whole process of creation through which each person generates, grows, transforms, and develops *naohinomitama* (the innermost pure spirit), making his or her spirit grow and become strong.
Nihonshoki	日本書紀	Chronicles of Japan, 720.
Norito	祝詞	Words that are spoken during ceremonies in order to address Kami, be it an announcement or a petition.
ofuda	お札	Card, made of paper or wood, carefully wrapped in white paper, with the name of some Kami written on it. This card functions as the "divided spirit" of the Kami of some shrine.

okage	お蔭	Sense of indebtedness, gratitude.
otodama	音霊	Spirit of the sounds.
reikai	霊界	World of spirit (see Chapter 7).
reijin	霊神	Different from *shinrei*: spirit who has reached rank of Kami through spiritual work.
seimei seichoku	清明正直	Clean bright right straight, the four types of *misogi* (see Chapter 4).
seisei kaiku	生成化育	Spiritual process of birth and growth, transformation, and development.
shimenawa	注連縄	Plaited straw rope to protect the shrine.
shinkai	神界	World of Kami (see Chapter 7).
shinrei	神霊	Different from *reijin*: the essence or nature of Kami that descends.
shuri kosei	修理固成	Spiritual process of renovation and maintenance.
tanden	丹田	Also: tantien; center of the true self; focus of attention in *chinkon* practice.
yaoyorozu no kami	八百万の神	Myriad other Kami.
yorishiro	依り代	Spiritual antenna, which receives the Spirit of Kami bestowing its radiating presence to the world here and now.
yukai	幽界	Hidden world (see Chapter 7).
yuniwa	斎庭	Purified yard or court.

Biographical Notes

Motohisa Yamakage

Motohisa Yamakage was born in 1925 and brought up in an old Shintoist family. At the age of eighteen he was initiated in the mysteries of Shinto, and in 1956 became the 79th Grand Master of Yamakage Shinto. He graduated in economics from Asia University of Tokyo.

Grand Master Yamakage has played a leading role in the promotion of Shinto on the world stage. Many of his essays have been translated into German, French, and English, and published in leading European magazines. The Grand Master has also collaborated with Western scholars and artists, such as Jean Herbert of the University of Geneva, and Michel Random of the French Broadcasting Corporation.

At the end of 2005, Motohisa Yamakage retired from his position as Grand Master and was succeeded by his son, Hitoyoshi Yamakage. His books (in Japanese) include *The Modern Significance of Shinto*, *Yoga and Shinto*, *Prayer and Miracle*, *An Introduction to Shinto* (five volumes), and a Japanese version of *The Essence of Shinto*.

Mineko Shinmura Gillespie & Gerald L. Gillespie

Mineko Shinmura was born in Tokushima, Japan. She studied Italian literature at Tokyo University of Foreign Studies and now lives in the United States. Mineko's major interests in recent years have been the study of esoteric Shinto and researching Japan's hidden history. Her husband, Gerald L. Gillespie, is Professor of Psychology at Kansas Wesleyan University.

Yoshitsugu Komuro

Yoshitsugu Komuro, MA, was born in 1951. He graduated in English literature at the Sophia University in Tokyo, after which he studied drama at Middlesex University in London and at the International Center of Theatre Research in Paris. As *kannushi* (Shinto master) of Yamakage Shinto in Japan, he was editor of the monthly magazine *Mezame*. Currently he is a teacher of English in Japan.

Paul de Leeuw

Paul de Leeuw, MA, was born in 1947 in The Netherlands. He graduated in Dutch literature and drama at the University of Leyden. He studied in Paris at the International Center of Theatre Research, where he met Master Yamakage. In 1979, he came to study at the Yamakage Shinto School Kireigu in Hamamatsu, and two years later founded the Japanese Dutch Shinzen Foundation. Paul is *kannushi* of the Shinto shrine in Amsterdam, The Netherlands. He is the author of *I am a Mirror* [*Ware wa Kagami Nari*] (Tokyo: Hakuba shuppan, 1980).

Aidan Rankin

Aidan Rankin, PhD, was born in 1966. He has an MA in modern history from Oxford University and gained his Masters and Doctorate in political science at the London School of Economics, where he lectured for several years. He has edited the political and cultural section of the *European Business Review* and is research consultant for the Economic Research Council in London. Aidan is a qualified stress counselor and author of *The Jain Path*: *Ancient Wisdom for the West* (Winchester /Washington: O Books, 2006).